READY CASH *IS* AVAILABLE
WHEN YOU NEED IT!

In many cases, all you have to do is ask for it! Learn how you can make use of the complete range of financial options available to you through your banker, real estate agent, employer, government, customers, tenants, family and partners, credit union or professional association, and others.

All sixty cash-raising options described in this book are legitimate. While all of them may not be right for you, some of them surely will be.

Trust deeds, brokers, IRAs, the FHA, leasebacks, refinancing, partnerships, bartering, sweat equity—the array of financial options can be pretty confusing without an experienced guide to take you carefully through the steps and to clarify the advantages, disadvantages, and special features of each option. Cris Molles provides that expertise in this exciting new guide book to solving your problems and creating a bright financial future.

60 WAYS TO
RAISE CASH
FAST!

Cris Molles

A DELL BOOK

Published by
Dell Publishing
a division of
Bantam Doubleday Dell Publishing Group, Inc.
666 Fifth Avenue
New York, New York 10103

ISBN: 0-440-21122-0

Printed in the United States of America

Published simultaneously in Canada

February 1992

10 9 8 7 6 5 4 3 2 1

Contents

60 WAYS TO
RAISE CASH
FAST!

INTRODUCTION

I first got the idea for this book a few years ago, when I was between jobs and had to raise cash in order to complete the purchase of a rental property. I learned a lot about raising money in a very short period of time. I currently have lines of credit worth over $80,000.

For the past eight years I have been the finance manager for several large Southern California automobile dealerships. My job is to negotiate with bankers to set up car loans for our customers, so I have learned even more about borrowing and raising money. Before I recommend one of these sixty ways to raise cash to customers who are short on funds, I make sure that they are familiar with the most basic personal finance transactions: getting a loan at a bank, establishing a line of credit, and clearing up bad credit.

I realize that some of the 60 ideas for raising cash in this book will not apply to everyone. I don't know anything about your current financial outlook—your assets, your credit, or your net worth. My hope is that you can find five or six ways to raise money that apply to your unique situation. I have used most of these plans successfully in my own financial dealings, and I can assure you that all of these plans are used every day, all over the United States, in order to raise millions of dollars. Some of the ideas in the book sound rather unusual, but you wouldn't be reading a book like this if you had a million bucks in the bank. You are reading this because you need to raise cash for some present or future purchase. I have tried to write about every legitimate way there is to raise money.

A lot of books (particularly in the real estate field) show you ways to raise money, but they forget to tell you about the drawbacks of each plan. I have tried to show both the benefits and the problems for each of the plans in my book. I may not have thought of all of them, but I have done my best to give you ideas and to point out the advantages and disadvantages of each.

A word on taxes: Most of these methods involve borrowing, so no extra taxes will be due, since borrowed money is not taxable. However, taxes may be due if you use any of the methods mentioned that involve a sale of an asset or any other type of gain. I have tried to point out most of the taxable situations. Since each case is different, you may want to talk to your accountant or tax preparer about your particular situation.

Also, many of these suggestions may require legal, accounting, or other professional assistance. This book is not intended to be a substitute for legal, accounting, or other specialized advice by a qualified professional. You should seek the services of a competent professional for legal or other expert assistance in any particular matter.

One final note—since there are so many ways to raise cash legitimately and honestly, it makes very little sense to do it dishonestly (such as by fraud, theft, deception, embezzlement, using a loan shark, and the like). Life's too short to spend any of it in jail. No matter how bad you need money, get it honestly!

Good luck in your financial future!

GETTING A LOAN AT A BANK

Probably the most obvious way to raise cash is through a loan from your local bank. Before you approach your friendly banker, take some time to prepare.

In order to make a loan, a bank needs to verify your employment and income, and possibly whether you own your own home and who holds the mortgage. Your banker will need to know what you want the loan money for (such as making investments, starting a business, buying a car, buying a house, paying off other bills, and so on). He needs to know how you intend to pay the money back: Will the proceeds come from the profits on your business or investment or from your regular salary? He will also need to know what kind of collateral you will be offering. Bankers generally need something to fall back on in case you don't repay the loan.

You want to have answers for any question your banker may come up with. It's amazing how many people go to banks with only a hazy idea of what they will do with the money they are trying to borrow. Let's look at a list of some of the things your lender may ask you for:

- Your current pay stub.
- Your previous year's 1040 or W-2. A lender wants to see how much money you've earned in the past.
- A business plan. This will show him what the money

is for—equipment, vehicles, advertising, and the like—and where the money will come from to pay back the loan.

- An appraisal of the property that will back the loan. Whether it is a home or rental property, the lender wants to see that you have assets to cover the loan.

- Previous credit information. Bring a list with the addresses and account numbers of all your current and previous creditors.

- If you are borrowing for the first time, it helps to bring a letter of introduction or a referral letter from a prominent member of the community or even from a customer in good standing with the bank. While not mandatory, such a letter will put the banker more at ease with you because you will not be a complete stranger off the street.

- Any contracts you may already have. If you are borrowing to start a business, show the lender that you already have customers for your product or service.

- Any other documents necessary to make your loan (such as purchase orders or contracts).

Be prepared, too, by looking as professional as you can. It makes sense to dress your best when going in to talk with your banker. Even if you're the type who never puts on a suit or a dress, do it this one time. Whether it's fair or not, the way you look affects the way your banker will judge you in his mind. If you are wearing a pair of shorts and a T-shirt, he may not want to loan you money, no matter how good the purpose. Put all the odds in your favor. Wear a suit or a dress. Look your best. Be prepared!

If you have proven yourself creditworthy in the past and you have a well-thought-out, complete plan for the purpose and repayment of a loan, your banker should look upon it very favorably.

BUILDING A $100,000 LINE OF CREDIT

After you have begun to establish your credit, building a large line of credit is simple. The way you start is to obtain a VISA or MasterCard. Your credit limit on the card might be anywhere from $500 to $1,000 at the beginning. Once you have the card, be sure to make your payments on time in order to create a good credit profile. After a period of six to twelve months of paying on time, ask the lending institution to raise your credit limit. Probably, it will approve this. It may even do this automatically on an annual basis for its good customers.

Next, apply for a couple more VISA or MasterCards. (The reason I keep referring to VISA and MasterCards is that they are the only cards you can get that can be cashed in, up to your credit limit, at any time.) Each new card you receive will probably have a $1,000-to-$2,000 limit. You can get as many cards as you feel comfortable with. If you got ten different cards, you would have a credit line worth between $10,000 and $20,000. As your credit history builds, the limits on your credit cards will increase too. Credit limits of $5,000 to 10,000 are quite common. (See plan number 2 for further details.)

The next step is to apply for an unsecured line of credit at your local bank. Lines of credit usually range from $5,000 to $10,000 for first-time borrowers. The credit requirements for lines of credit are a little stiffer than for regular credit cards (see numbers 3 and 4 for details). By developing credit lines at several different banks, you could easily build up another $20,000 to $50,000.

This plan may take several months or even years to carry out, but eventually you can build up a very substantial line of credit that is available to you at any time for any purpose you choose.

Note that just because you can build up a $50,000 or $100,000 credit line doesn't mean you should go out and blow it all. Use this money for a productive purpose—financing an education, buying a home or other real estate, or starting a business. Try to find investments that will return at least as much as your payments on your credit lines, if not more. A large line of credit can be used as leverage to greatly increase your wealth, but it can be quite a burden if you use it foolishly.

How To Clean Up Bad Credit

Where do you begin if your credit now is poor? Should you use one of those credit cleanup services? Is there anything you can do yourself? This may come as a surprise, but it's easier than you may think to clean up bad credit.

There are companies all over the country that will guarantee to clean up your bad credit for a fee of $250 to $500. All they do for their money is send out a deluge of letters to your previous creditors asking that your bad credit rating be eliminated from the various credit files. You can do that yourself and save the money!

If you currently have outstanding credit balances that are delinquent, pay them off completely or make new payment arrangements that you can live with comfortably. No banker will ever lend you money if you are not current with all your existing creditors.

Call your various creditors and make arrangements to pay them. Work out payment schedules that you can live with. Send letters to them verifying what you agreed to over the phone, and keep a copy for your records. You have to get current with your creditors before you can begin to repair the damage to your credit rating.

Once your payments are up to date with your current creditors, the next step is to straighten out your credit file. Everyone in the United States with any previous credit has a credit rating with one of the major credit-reporting services (such as TRW, TransUnion, or CBI/Equifax). Before most lenders will make you a loan, they will look at your credit report to see how promptly you have paid your previous creditors. If your credit report shows late payments or defaults to previous creditors, most potential new lenders will pass on making you a loan or extending new credit to you.

To clean up your credit report, write a letter to the credit-reporting companies. Their addresses are listed below. If you have recently been turned down for credit based on information in your credit file, you will receive a letter telling you where you can obtain a free copy of your credit report and how to update any incorrect information.

If there is incorrect information in your file, by all means correct it in writing to the reporting companies. If you want, you can even include a letter explaining the reason for your credit problems (a layoff, a prolonged sickness, a disability, a death in the family, a divorce) that can be included on your credit report for all future lenders to read.

The phone numbers and addresses of the major credit reporting services are as follows:

TRW
P.O. Box 749029
Dallas, TX 75374
($8 charge for report)
(714) 385-7000

TransUnion
1561 East Orangethorpe
Fullerton, CA 92631
($15 for a single report, $30 for a joint husband and wife
report, or $8 and $16 respectively for California residents)
(213) 620-8530

CBI/Equifax
130 South State College Boulevard
Suite 100
Brea, CA 92621
($8 charge for report)
(714) 972-2360

To receive a copy of your credit report, just send along
a brief letter requesting your report and include the following information: your full name (including your mid-
dle initial and any Jr. or Sr.), your complete address (along
with all addresses for the past five years), your Social Security number, and your date of birth. Sign and date the
letter, and send it along with the appropriate fee to the
addresses listed above. If you have been turned down for
credit or employment based on information contained in
the credit file, the report will be sent to you free of charge.
Simply send the turndown letter along with the other information. The reports will be sent to you within about two
weeks.

Once you have done all you can to clean up your credit
report, sit back and relax. You may not be able to eliminate
all of your derogatory credit history, but time is on your
side. Eventually, some of the bad credit that is now showing on your credit report will drop off. This will clean up
many of your bad ratings. Creditors tend to regard the
most recent credit ratings as the most accurate. As your

bad credit gets older (one to three years old), it will count against you less. Potential creditors will pay more attention to the new credit you have established.

But how do you go about building up new, good credit ratings? The best way is to start all over, as though you were applying for credit for the first time. Visit your local banker and offer to keep $500 in a secured account if he will grant you a VISA or MasterCard with a $250 limit. Explain that your previous credit problems have all been taken care of and are behind you. You are interested in reestablishing some new credit. Everyone wins with this type of arrangement. You get the VISA card, and the banker gets a new $500 deposit account and a new cardholder. (See number 57 for further details.) Next, you may want to try to get credit cards from a couple of small department stores in your area. If you do charge anything on them, be sure to pay it off on time according to your credit agreement. It doesn't do you any good to straighten out your credit, then begin making late payments all over again.

After a year or two of reestablishing your credit, you may be able to qualify for a car loan. Since you will still have some previous bad credit on your record, you may have to put down a large down payment (30 to 50 percent of the selling price) and pay a much higher interest rate than a preferred borrower would. Don't worry about it. This is simply your penalty for having had bad credit previously. Eventually, you will again be a preferred borrower.

Keep in mind that every time you apply for credit, an "inquiry" from the potential creditor will appear on your credit rating. An inquiry is simply a listing of who has requested your credit report. If you send out twenty credit applications, your credit report will have twenty inquiries. These inquiries will stay on your report for one to two years, so it's wise not to try to apply for too much credit all at once. Future potential creditors will see this and assume (correctly) that you are desperate to get credit and are applying everywhere. This may scare them off. Try not to apply to more than five or six creditors a year. Try to keep the number of inquiries as low as possible.

That's basically all there is to repairing bad credit and starting over. Remember that it takes time. New lenders are not going to loan you money overnight. You have to build up a new credit profile. Make your current payments on time for a year or so before you try to get a lot of new credit. And when you do get a second chance, don't blow it. Make your payments in full and on time! Credit is one of those things that you don't really appreciate until it's gone.

THE 60 WAYS . . .

#1. Plan Ahead

You may have bought this book because you need fast cash. That's fine. This book provides dozens of ways in which you can raise money virtually overnight.

But that's not the main thing I want you to learn. I want to show you that it always helps to plan ahead. Build your credit in advance so that it will be available when you need it. You've probably heard the old saying that banks want to lend money only to people who don't need it. That saying may have a grain of truth in it. The best credit risks don't need the money because they take the time to establish credit before it is necessary.

The worst time to borrow money is when you are desperate. The worst time to raise cash is when you need it tomorrow, or else. You don't want to beg for a loan at any rate or on any terms. You want to be in command of your own destiny.

How can you begin to establish credit now? Well, first

get your financial affairs in order. Open a checking and savings account. This establishes a banking relationship and shows a potential lender that you have stability. If you are willing to set down roots, a lender feels that you are more creditworthy because you probably won't get up and leave town. Next, apply for a VISA or MasterCard at that bank. Talk to the loan officers. Often they have special programs for beginning cardholders. Once you have a credit card with your bank, apply for a few department store cards. When you have established those, you can probably qualify for a small personal loan or a car loan.

Build up your credit in small steps. It won't happen overnight. Work on it a little bit at a time. Then, you will have credit available when you need it. You won't be left out in the cold in an emergency.

#2. Cash in Your Credit Cards

One of the fastest ways to raise several thousand dollars quickly is to tap your credit cards. By that, I mean that you can go into your local bank and draw out money against your credit card up to your limit.

Let's say, for example, that you have a VISA or Master-Card with a $2,000 limit. You can draw that money out by asking your bank to let you have a cash advance against the card. You may not be able to draw out the entire amount in one day—many banks have a $500 or $1,000 limit on credit card cash advances. I think you can see how easy it is to raise cash in this manner.

Now let's take it one step further. Assume that you have established ten VISA cards with different financial institutions, and each has a $2,000 to $3,000 limit. (This is not as far-fetched as it may sound. Millions of people have four or five different VISA or MasterCards.) You can tap each of these cards to its limit and raise $20,000 to $30,000 in a matter of a few days, without any applications or waiting for a bank's approval!

HOW MUCH YOU CAN RAISE

This is limited only by the number of credit cards you have and the limit on each card. Conceivably, you could establish VISAS or MasterCards with dozens of different banks, making your total line of credit $20,000 to $50,000 or more!

HOW FAST

You can usually tap your credit cards to their maximum in a matter of days.

CREDIT NEEDED

Since you are dealing with conventional lenders, good credit is necessary to obtain VISA and MasterCard charge accounts.

ADVANTAGES

You don't have to deal with lenders (once you have the cards), so there is no lag time while you wait for credit approvals. This method takes some advance planning; you must set up several credit cards, and check with your local banks to see how much cash advance you can take on each card per day. Overall, this is one of the best ways to raise cash quickly and simply. I have even heard of people using their credit cards to finance small business startups.

DISADVANTAGES

Since most credit card interest is in the 16 to 22 percent range, this can be a very expensive way to borrow money, compared with normal bank loans. Also, the monthly payment may be as much as one-twentieth of the outstanding balance plus interest. On a $20,000 balance, this can equal $1,000 per month or more. (With a conventional loan, the payback period is much longer, which reduces your monthly payment.) Investigate beforehand to make sure you can handle the debt load you will incur with this type of borrowing.

#3. Line of Credit

One great way to raise large sums of money fast is to use lines of credit. For consumers these are relatively new on the financial scene. Once you have established one, it can be used at any time for any purpose you choose, and you don't have to pay any interest until you draw on it.

Here is how you go about securing a line of credit. Call several banks in your local area. Find out which of them offer lines of credit—not all banks do. Find out what their terms are, what they base their credit decisions on, and the amount of their annual fees. Line up several banks, and send applications to them at approximately the same time. That way, you may be accepted for lines of credit at several banks at once.

A bank usually bases a line of credit on your previous credit history, your ability to pay, and your assets. If your previous credit has been paid satisfactorily, if you have a decent job with some discretionary income (money not needed to pay monthly bills), and if you own a few things (like a house, cars, or property), you have a good chance of getting a line of credit.

An individual line of credit can range anywhere from $2,500 to $50,000 or more. Once you are approved, you will receive a book of checks. You can use these checks at any time for any purpose, and you pay interest only on the outstanding balance. Generally, you are required to pay only back interest plus a small amount of the loan each month, making the payments very reasonable. Some lines of credit require a monthly payment that covers only the interest accrued. That would come to approximately $100 per month on a $10,000 balance. And since most line-of-credit holders are preferred borrowers, the interest charge is usually just a few percentage points over the prime rate, making this a very inexpensive way to borrow.

Another advantage to lines of credit is that they are usually unsecured. This means that they are not backed by anything except your promise to repay and your previous credit track record. You don't have to tie up any of your assets to secure the loan!

How Much You Can Raise

This depends entirely on your ability to repay (your income), your previous credit history, and your assets. Most banks allow lines of credit of approximately one-sixth to one-tenth of your assets (home equity, income property equity, cars, furnishings, boats, stocks, bonds, money in the bank, and so on, minus all your debts). If your assets are $50,000, you would qualify for credit of between $5,000 and $9,000, depending on the bank's lending criteria.

How Fast

Lines of credit are established within seven to ten working days, on the average. It's a good idea to have lines of credit set up before you need them. Keep them in reserve, just in case.

Credit Needed

Since lines of credit may be for very substantial amounts and are usually unsecured by any assets, your credit generally has to be excellent to qualify for them.

Advantages

To reiterate, the advantages of credit lines are many. You can use them for any purpose you choose; you use them only when you need them, so you are not paying interest on them all the time. They are unsecured, so that if you default, you probably will not lose your house, car, or other assets. The monthly payments are small, and as you pay a credit line down, you can use it over and over again up to your limit. For example, let's say that your credit line is $10,000, and you use all of it as a down payment on a piece of rental property. After a few months, you pay your credit line back down to $6,000. You now have $4,000 left that you can use again, without filling in another application or waiting for loan approval.

Disadvantages

But there are also drawbacks. First, lines of credit are usually set up with adjustable interest rates, so if the rates rise, your payments rise too. Second, they can usually be called in at the discretion of the lender (for example, the lender decides that you are no longer a worthy credit risk). If this happens, you will be required to pay back the balance in a short, specified period. This may make your payments much higher than they had previously been. Don't ever extend yourself out so far that you cannot take on a larger payment without defaulting. And finally, as with any type of credit, you really have to control your use of credit lines. Try to use them for investment purposes, not for frivolous items that will be forgotten in a short time.

#4. Expand Your Line of Credit

Once you have set up lines of credit at several banks, you can raise even more money by having the limit on those lines increased. Most banks will be willing to go along with this idea if you have proven yourself to be creditworthy and can support the payments that a larger line of credit could require. Many banks automatically increase the credit limits of their good customers.

Here's how you can expedite a credit line increase. After you have paid satisfactorily on your credit line for several months, contact the bank about increasing the line. It's a good idea to do a little groundwork first. Give the bank an updated net worth statement to show that you can support a larger credit line. If you have had an increase in salary or a promotion, don't hesitate to bring that up. It also helps to outline a plan that explains to your banker why you need an expanded line of credit and what you will do with it. For example, if you will be using the funds to purchase rental property or some other solid investment, type up a letter that states your intentions. This will show your banker how responsible you are and that you won't use the money for a frivolous purpose. The more documentation you provide, the better. This gives your lender ammunition to approve your credit line increase.

If you have five lines of credit at various banks and you can expand each one by only $2,000, you will have an increase of $10,000 of spending power. This is quite an amplification of your credit.

How Much You Can Raise

This depends on how many lines you currently have and by how much you can increase each one. I have increased my lines of credit by $5,000 at a time. You may be able to raise that much or more.

How Fast

If you have all the documentation necessary, an expanded line of credit can usually be arranged in a week or less.

Credit Needed

See number 3.

Advantages

See number 3.

Disadvantages

See number 3, then multiply.

#5. Preapproved Loan and Credit Line

As you build up good credit, you will begin to receive offers for preapproved loans and credit lines in the mail. These are sent out by large financial institutions that buy lists of people who have good credit, or lists of people who've just qualified to buy a new house or car. They may send out literally hundreds of thousands of offers of preapproved loans and credit lines every month.

You may want to take advantage of these offers. Even if you don't need the money right now, put the letter away for use later. If you do want the loan now, simply sign in a few places and mail the card or letter back. There is usually a small annual fee involved, and the interest rates are usually not the lowest around since the companies send out thousands of these letters to people of all types of credit risk. (If your credit is excellent, then the higher rate you are paying is subsidizing other people's defaulted loans. If your credit is marginal, you are probably happy to be paying any rate in order to borrow money.)

After you return the card or letter, you will probably receive a batch of checks that you can use for any purpose, up to the amount of your credit line. The interest doesn't begin accumulating until you actually use the checks. This is a great feature! You have a credit line on tap for any purpose—and you don't begin paying for it until you need it!

How Much You Can Raise

The amounts are generally between $1,500 and $10,000.

How Fast

You will normally receive your checks within a month of returning your preapproved loan letter.

Credit Needed

Since these letters and offers are sent to homeowners and other good credit risks, your credit rating has to be pretty good to be included in these mailings.

Advantages

These types of loans are very convenient to get (you never even have to leave your home!) and very easy to use— just write a check. The interest and payments don't begin until you use your checks, so you can put them away for future use, and they'll be available anytime you need them. (You will probably have to pay a small annual fee to keep the line of credit open.) You could even build up several of these lines of credit and use them for one large purchase, such as a down payment on a house or rental property.

Disadvantages

The interest rates for preapproved loans and credit lines are generally several percentage points higher than they are on other types of loans that you may be able to get. Also, these offers come in the mail on a very irregular basis. You can't depend on one to come to you just when you need it for some planned purchase.

#6. Borrow Against Your Life Insurance

If you have a whole life insurance policy in force, you may be able to borrow money against it. There are two main types of life insurance: whole life and term. Term insurance is simply a policy that pays if you die. The premiums usually escalate as you get older. With whole life, you generally pay a level annual premium that is based on your age at the time you got the policy. Whole life insurance also builds up a "cash value." This is money that you can have or borrow at any time.

Here's how it works. If you have had a whole life policy for a few years, you have probably built up a small cash value. You can have this money simply by asking your insurance agent to fill out a request form. You will have your money a couple of weeks after this is turned in. You can use the money for anything you wish. You don't ever have to pay it back. If you do choose to pay it back, the interest rate is usually very reasonable (5 to 8 percent). If you die after you take out your cash value, your heirs' proceeds are reduced by that amount. For example, if you have a $50,000 whole life policy with a current cash value of $2,000, you can have the entire $2,000 now, but if you die without paying it back, the insurance will pay off only $48,000. To many people, this seems like a reasonable exchange.

How Much You Can Raise

This completely depends upon how large your cash value is. This is determined by how long your policy has been in force. The declaration sheet on the front of your policy shows you how much cash you build up for every year the insurance is in effect.

How Fast

You can generally get your money in five to ten working days.

Credit Needed

Your credit rating doesn't matter, since you are in effect borrowing from the proceeds of your own policy.

Advantages

Using the cash value from a life insurance policy is one of the best ways to raise cash fast. The money belongs to you. You can choose to pay it back, but if you don't, it is simply deducted from the net insurance proceeds when you die. Taking out your cash value is like having your cake and eating it too. One thing that the insurance companies don't tell you is that unless you take out your cash value, it's gone when you die. They only pay off the face value of the policy, not the face amount plus the cash value.

Disadvantages

The only disadvantage to pulling out your life insurance

cash value is that the policy payout is reduced by that amount if you should die. That's a gamble that most people seem willing to take.

#7. Margin Your Stock

You may have stock that, for one reason or another, you don't want to sell. (Perhaps you were given it by a relative and it has sentimental value, or perhaps it will pay a dividend soon.) But you can still pull out money if you need it. One way to do this is to margin your stock.

If you own shares in a stock that sells for over $5 per share, you can margin, or borrow against, that stock. Here's how margin works. You can borrow up to one-half of the value of the stock. If you have five hundred shares of a $10 stock, you could borrow $2,500. You are actually borrowing from your brokerage and using the stock as collateral.

If your stock falls by more than 25 percent of its value, you will get a margin call. This means that your brokerage will require you to come up with some money because now it is loaning you over 50 percent of the value of the stock. In our example, if your stock falls from $10 to $7.50 per share, your brokerage will have loaned you $2,500 against only $3,750 in stock. You are required to get that level down to 50 percent again. You can do this either by coming up with money on your own or by letting the brokerage sell some of your shares in order to reduce your loan amount.

How Much You Can Raise

You can borrow up to one-half the value of your shares.

How Fast

Margin accounts can usually be set up by making a call to your broker. There is usually a seven-day settlement period before you receive your money.

Credit Needed

A good credit rating isn't necessary because the loan from the brokerage is 200 percent collateralized (the security for the loan—your stocks—have twice the value of the loan they are making you).

Advantages

If you want to raise money without selling your stock, this is one way to do it. It allows you to hold your shares and still pull some cash out. The interest that you pay on your margin account is usually quite low, often several points below normal bank rates.

Disadvantages

There are many disadvantages to margining your stock. First, it is very risky. If the market value of your stock drops dramatically (as in October 1987), you will receive a margin call. If you can't come up with the money you need, your stock will be sold to pay off the debt and accumulated interest. For this reason, you have to have substantial assets to qualify for a margin account. Brokerages don't want people with few assets to get involved with margining stock. They want investors with some capital behind them who can weather any financial storms that may arise. For this reason, some people may not qualify for a margin account. Also, marginable stock has to be priced over $5 per share. There are a few other minor requirements too. But the stocks that you own may not be over $5 per share, or they may not qualify for some other reason.

#8. The Sixty-Day IRA Switch

Many people look upon their individual retirement account (IRA) as money put away for retirement that they can't touch until they are fifty-nine and a half years old. Well, if you need money fast and you have an IRA account, there are a couple of ways to have your cake and eat it too.

The first of these ways is called the Sixty-day switch. According to the law, once every year, you can switch your IRA from one financial institution to another. After you close your existing IRA account, you have sixty days in which to open your new IRA account at the bank of your choice. This interim period is actually a sixty-day interest-free loan.

Let's say, for example, that you need $5,000 for an investment, and that you don't want to borrow the money from a bank. You know that you have $5,000 coming in the next two months, but you need the money immediately for an investment. You have more than $5,000 in your IRA account. You can simply close the IRA account at your present institution and use the money for the investment you were looking at. Then when the money you were expecting arrives, start up your new IRA at a new bank within sixty days. You have just given yourself an interest-free "swing loan" (a short-term loan to make purchases or investments, knowing that other funds will be coming through for you shortly). Note that since the tax laws are always subject to change or modification, you should check with your accountant or other appropriate professional to see if there were any changes in the tax laws regarding this type of transaction.

How Much You Can Raise

This is limited only by how much you have in your IRA account.

How Fast

You can close out your IRA account in a few minutes and have the money in your hands immediately, or at most in a day or two.

Credit Needed

Your credit rating doesn't matter since you are not applying for a loan.

Advantages

The advantages to this plan are many. First, there is no delay. You can have the funds as fast as you can get down to your local bank. There is no application to fill out, no loan officer to talk to, no credit committee to worry about. You are using your own funds, so you have complete control. Second, there are no costs such as interest, points, or loan fees. The only cost you may incur is a small account closure fee, which is usually $25 or $30. As long as you are fairly certain that you will have the money to replace your IRA in sixty days, this is one of the fastest, cheapest, and simplest ways to raise cash fast.

DISADVANTAGES

The main disadvantages to the sixty-day IRA switch is the two-month time frame. It may put severe restrictions on when you can use this kind of funding. Sixty days go by awfully fast, and if you don't have the funds to begin your IRA at another institution, there are two penalties. The first is that you have to include the money you took out of your old IRA as income on your tax return for that year. There is also a 10 percent penalty imposed by the IRS. So if you close your IRA at one bank and do not open one at another bank within sixty days, the money will be fully taxable on your 1040 tax form, along with a 10 percent penalty.

#9. Using Your IRA Money

Most people look upon their IRA account as money to be used strictly for their retirement. They don't realize that they can use a large IRA nest egg at any time, for any purpose.

In number 8, I showed you how you can use your IRA money with no penalty as long as you make a transfer within sixty days. But what if you need money for a longer period?

If you need money for an extended period of time, your IRA account is still a good place to look for it. When you withdraw money from an IRA account (other than for a sixty-day transfer), you have to pay a 10 percent tax penalty on that amount in the year that it is withdrawn. This is reasonable, since you were able to deduct your IRA contributions each year on your previous tax returns. You also have to add the amount withdrawn to your taxable income for that year. For example, if you were to withdraw $5,000 from your IRA account, you would owe a $500 penalty, and $5,000 would be added to your taxable income for that year. Even with the penalties involved, however, this can be a quick, inexpensive way to raise cash.

You may even be able to take money from your IRA for certain expenses—such as major medical expenses or certain education expenses—without paying any penalty at all. The laws regarding this type of penalty-free withdrawal are constantly changing, so it is a good idea to call your local IRS office for an update. If you are using the funds for one of the special purposes, you might as well take advantage of this penalty exclusion.

HOW MUCH YOU CAN RAISE

This depends on how much you have in your IRA account. You can withdraw 100 percent of it.

HOW FAST

You can get the money as fast as it takes you to go to your bank and ask for an IRA transfer. You have to fill out a form for the IRS, but the financial institution should have your money ready immediately.

CREDIT NEEDED

Your credit rating doesn't matter since you are not applying for a loan.

ADVANTAGES

When you take money out of your IRA account, you are simply borrowing from yourself. In other words, you are not incurring any new debt—you are simply withdrawing money from a special type of savings account. You can get the money immediately or as fast as the next banking day. This type of withdrawal makes the most sense if you are now earning less than you were earning when you made the IRA contributions. You got the tax savings when your income was higher, and you pay the tax penalties now when your income is lower. This is a good way to save money for some future investment and get tax savings along the way.

DISADVANTAGES

First of all, you have to pay the 10 percent penalty on the money you withdrew, plus add the money to your taxable income at year's end. That can make an IRA withdrawal a bit costly. Also, your IRA account is designed to be a personal Social Security plan. The government developed these plans and gave them terrific tax savings in order to get people to depend on themselves in old age, not on government programs. When you draw this money out before your retirement, in many ways you are defeating the whole idea.

#10. IRA Secured Loan

You have an IRA account, but you don't want to touch it to raise cash. Instead, you can get a loan secured against that account. This type of loan is very easy to qualify for and set up, since the bank is making a totally secured loan. The bank puts a lock on your IRA account, and you get the loan at a point or two more than the interest that you are being paid on the IRA itself. Therefore, if you have, say, $6,000 in your IRA account and you are receiving 7 percent on your money, the bank will probably lend you up to $6,000 at 8 to 9 percent, with your IRA account as collateral.

This is a very good way to raise some quick cash, at a very low interest rate, without disturbing your IRA money and losing the great tax benefits.

How Much You Can Raise

A lender will usually allow you to borrow against 100 percent of the amount in your IRA.

How Fast

This type of loan can be set up within a couple of days.

Credit Needed

Credit should not really be a factor, since the bank is simply loaning your money that is 100 percent secured by your own deposits.

Advantages

This is an excellent way to raise money. You can borrow at a very low interest rate, and the loan is backed by your own assets, so there is very little chance of a default and a resulting bad credit rating. Most of the time, borrowing against your IRA makes a lot more sense than taking the money out of the IRA account completely, paying penalties, and losing tax benefits.

Disadvantages

Many people cannot borrow large amounts of cash in this manner because they don't have substantial balances in their IRA accounts. Another disadvantage is that since you are locking in your IRA as security for the loan, you can't switch it to other financial institutions to take advantage of higher rates.

#11. Take Out
a Second Trust Deed

If you own a home or other property, you can probably raise some cash fast by taking out a second trust deed, or a second mortgage as it is known in some states. Acquiring a second trust deed is simply borrowing additional money against your property. The loan amount you owe to your original lender is called your first trust deed. If you borrow more, the new lender has second right of claim on your property in case of a default—hence the name "second."

Here is how you go about getting a second trust deed. Look through your newspaper's real estate section or the phone book for real estate loans. Most financial institutions will lend on either a first or a second trust deed (although the rates and other fees are a little higher on the second because of the extra risk involved for the lender). After you apply for the loan, the lender will send out an appraiser to verify that you have enough equity in your property to qualify for a loan. Financial institutions usually lend out a maximum of only 75 to 80 percent of the value of real estate. So, for example, if your property is worth $120,000 and you owe approximately $75,000 on the first mortgage, you could probably borrow another $15,000 to $21,000 depending on the lender's criteria ($120,000 × .80 = $96,000 minus your first mortgage of $75,000 = $21,000).

You will also have to meet other requirements. The lender will verify your employment and figure a debt ratio to make sure you can afford the extra payments according to its guidelines. The lender will then check your credit to make sure you have paid all your other debts on time and have built up a good credit rating.

If you meet all these criteria, you should have no problem getting your loan. If, however, you have had credit problems in the past or don't otherwise qualify under "normal" lending guidelines, you may qualify for a loan from an "equity lender." Equity lenders are less concerned about your credit, job, and income than about the equity in your home or property. They are willing to take additional risk and make loans to those with marginal credit, so they will usually only lend up to about 70 percent of the value of your property. This may eliminate a lot of potential borrowers. An equity lender will also charge additional points on the loan and set a much higher interest rate than standard lenders.

How Much You Can Raise

This depends on the value of your real estate and how much you already owe—that is, your equity. You may be able to borrow up to 80 percent of it.

How Fast

A second trust deed usually takes about four weeks to come through because the lender has to process all the loan paperwork and order a title search. The title search document verifies that you don't already owe money on your property that you are concealing from the lender, and that you actually have the authority to secure loans on the property. After the loan is approved and the title search is complete, you will sign the loan documents and then wait three days for the money. During this "cooling off" period, you have a chance to back out of the loan with no penalty if you decide that is isn't such a good idea.

Credit Needed

You will need a good credit rating to use a standard lender. If you have a poor credit rating, you will have to use an equity lender and pay higher points and interest on the loan.

Advantages

Depending on your equity, you may be able to raise more money this way that just about any other way. The interest rates are generally pretty reasonable—10 to 13 percent currently. The loan periods may be stretched out for anywhere from ten to thirty years, which can lower your payments dramatically.

Disadvantages

If for some reason you cannot make your payments, your lender has the right to foreclose on your property. Generally, lenders do not like to take back a property. After all, they are in the loan business, not the real estate business. Therefore, they may be willing to work with you if there is a problem. Then again, they may not. Also, you usually have to pay closing costs and points on a second trust deed loan. A point equals one percent of the loan amount. If the lender charged you four points on a $25,000 second trust deed loan, the points alone would cost $1,000! The points and other costs involved can make this type of loan very expensive.

#12. Sell Your
Second Trust Deed

After selling a piece of real estate and agreeing to carry back a second trust deed, you will be besieged with offers to sell it. The fact that you hold a second trust deed becomes a matter of public record. Buyers of trust deeds comb these files to find holders of trust deeds and then send them offers to buy. Unfortunately, these offers do not equal the face value of the deed. In order to sell a trust deed before its term expires, you usually have to sell at a discount. Assuming you don't want to hold a trust deed and receive a monthly payment but would rather get a large lump sum instead, here's how to sell it.

Let's say that you own a second trust deed (called a second mortgage in some states) for $10,000, paying interest only at 12 percent for three years. Your income from this trust deed is $100 per month. Buyers of trust deeds usually offer only 70 to 85 percent of the face value of the note, so a $10,000 trust deed will usually sell for $7,000 to

$8,500 on the open market. If the buyer can purchase the note for, let's say, $7,500, the monthly return on his or her investment will equal 16 percent—plus, he or she will receive the full $10,000 at the end of the term, making a $2,500 profit! These types of returns are why so many investors like to buy discounted trust deeds.

You may be able to shop around between several trust deed buyers and negotiate a better deal than the example I've given. By all means, check with several different buyers! The difference can mean thousands of dollars to you—definitely worth the time it takes to make a few extra phone calls.

How Much You Can Raise

You can raise 70 to 85 percent of the face value of the note.

How Fast

Usually within ten working days (since the buyer of the note has to transfer the title and take care of other legal matters).

Credit Needed

Your own credit isn't important. The trust deed buyer is mainly interested in the credit record of the person paying the note.

Advantages

This is a very quick way to raise cash without having to borrow. You are simply selling a note to another investor. If you have sold a property and don't really want to carry back any paper, this is a good way to get your cash fast!

Disadvantages

The main disadvantage with selling a note before it is due is that you have to discount 15 percent, 20 percent, or even 30 percent in some cases (depending on the terms of the note, the location and condition of the property, and so on). This means that a trust deed worth $10,000 at maturity is worth only $7,000 to $8,500 now. Also, if you sell the note, you will no longer receive the monthly income from it. This may be the right choice for you if you need a large amount of cash immediately as opposed to a small monthly payment for several years.

#13. Borrow Against Your Second Trust Deed

Let's say that you need to raise some cash and you own a second trust deed from a property you have sold. You don't need a lot of money, and you don't want to sell your trust deed to someone at a large discount. Well, you may be able to borrow against your second trust deed even if it isn't scheduled to pay off for several years. Here's how you would go about it.

Look in the real estate section of your local newspaper. In most large metropolitan papers, there is a section called "Money to Lend" or "Second Trust Deeds." Go down the listing. There will be offers to buy and sell second trust deeds. There probably will also be a couple of ads from lenders who will let you borrow against your second trust deed without selling it outright.

If you don't see any ads in the paper, look in the phone book under "Real Estate Loans" or "Mortgage Lenders." Read the ads carefully. Usually, there are several lenders listed who will loan you money using your second trust deed as collateral. The great thing about this type of loan is that you can usually borrow money at the same rate or a bit higher rate than you are currently receiving on your second trust deed. Therefore, your payments will be just a few bucks more than you are receiving on your second trust deed.

For example, let's assume that you are currently receiving 10 percent interest on a $10,000 second trust deed that you are holding. If you are being paid interest only, you are receiving $83.33 monthly. Now you use the second trust deed as collateral on a $7,000 loan from a lender, and you arrange an interest-only loan at 13 percent. Your monthly payment is $75.83. So you borrow $7,000 and actually pay out less than you are currently receiving on the note itself. Not bad, huh?

How Much You Can Raise

This depends on how large your second trust deed is. Generally, you can borrow 60 to 75 percent of the value of the second trust deed.

How Fast

You can probably have the money in your hands within ten working days. There may be a three-day "cooling off" period before you can receive the money. This is for your benefit so you have time to reconsider the loan before you actually get the funds.

Credit Needed

Since you are basically setting up a secured loan (the second trust deed and the actual real estate back it up), your credit rating is not important and probably won't even be a factor in the loan process. As a matter of fact, the lender will probably be more interested in the credit and payment record of the individual who is paying you on the note, because if you default on the loan, the bank will own your second trust deed and will receive all future income from the note.

ADVANTAGES

There are many advantages to this type of borrowing. First of all, you can get the money now, regardless of when the second trust deed actually matures. Second, the costs involved with this type of borrowing are minimal, as shown by the example above. Third, you can get cash without selling your second trust deed, which usually involves a 15 to 25 percent discount. (Therefore, a $10,000 trust deed may fetch only $7,500 to $8,500 when sold outright.)

DISADVANTAGES

As with any other type of secured loan, if you can't make your payments, the lender can take over the collateral—in this case, the second trust deed on the property. Also, you have to make your payments to the lender whether or not you are being paid on your second trust deed. If the new owner of your property fails to make his payments to you, you have to go through the legal hassle of foreclosure, which can be costly, while contining to make payments on your second-trust-deed-secured loan. Finally, there may be points involved in getting this type of loan. A point equals 1 percent of the value of the loan. If a lender charges you four points on an $8,000 loan, you would end up paying $320 in loan charges. This amount is usually deducted up front, so you actually receive only $7,680 from the lender. The lender may also charge you other "junk fees" that could raise the cost of the loan. You have to decide for yourself whether these extra costs still make the loan worthwhile for you.

#14. Cut Your Withholding

A lot of people like to get a big tax return at the end of the year. But they do not realize that they could have used that money throughout the year. If you have squeezed all the cash out of every source you can think of, try this plan. It's like getting an immediate raise.

Let's say that your weekly salary is $800. By the time you get your check, the government has taken out 25 to 30 percent or more in withholding taxes, leaving you with only $500 to $600. There is very little you can do about your Social Security taxes, but you can cut down on some of your other payroll deductions.

The government furnishes your employer with guidelines as to how much state and federal taxes to withhold out of your salary every week. These are only suggestions. You can actually set the amount that you want withheld yourself. You can do this in one of two ways. The first is to claim many more exemptions than you actually have. This reduces the amount that the government suggests your employer withhold. The second way, which is simpler, is to fill out a new W-2 form specifying the exact percentage of your income that you want withheld by your employer. This is very easy to do, and your employer should not mind.

If your salary is $800 per week, and the state and federal taxes withheld equal 20 percent, this comes to $160 per week, $688 per month, or about $8,300 per year. You can see that reducing your withholding to 10 percent or less can substantially add to your income. And it is completely legal!

How Much You Can Raise

This depends on your income and how much you are presently having withheld. As you can see by the example above, the savings can add up to hundreds of dollars per month.

How Fast

You will begin to see the savings as soon as you receive your next paycheck.

Credit Needed

Your credit rating doesn't matter since you are not applying for a loan.

Advantages

Cutting your withholding is simple. You fill out a small form, and immediately you begin receiving a larger paycheck. A larger chunk of your income will be going to you rather than the government. If your income is high enough, you may realize an increase of $100 to $200 per week!

Disadvantages

The main problem with this plan is that you have to be absolutely sure that enough taxes are still taken out of your check to cover your tax bill at the end of the year. This requires you to carefully monitor your tax situation throughout the year and to have the discipline to make changes when necessary. It does you very little good to receive an extra $100 per week on your paycheck, but then owe a $5,000 tax bill on April 15. Also, if less than 90 percent of your final tax bill has been withheld during the year, you will owe the IRS a small penalty (usually 5 to 11 percent) of the amount owed. It is a good idea to talk with your tax preparer or accountant before reducing your withholding, and to monitor any changes with him or her as the year progresses.

#15. Refinance Your Car or Other Vehicle

Do you hold the title to your car? Is it a late model? Do you own it outright with no liens against it? If so, you may be able to borrow against it to raise cash.

In order to borrow against your car, it has to be relatively new. Most financial institutions will lend money only on cars that are in the *Kelley Blue Book* or other automotive price guide. These guides usually list only cars going back six or seven years. A lender will usually lend 75 to 100 percent of the wholesale value of your vehicle. (Wholesale value is what a dealer would buy your car for—retail value is what he would sell it for, after reconditioning.) For example, if your car has a low "book" (wholesale) value of $3,000, you could probably borrow anywhere from $2,250 to $3,000. Your loan-payback period would probably be twenty-four to forty-eight months; the smaller the loan, the shorter the payback period. On these types of loans, your payments are generally very reasonable.

Just about anybody with reasonable credit can obtain an auto loan. They are offered by banks, credit unions, thrifts and loans, and finance companies. Rates on this type of used-car loan are generally in the higher range (15 to 22 percent, depending on which state you live in). Shop around for the best deal as interest rates vary considerably among different institutions.

Just as you can refinance your car if you hold the title, you can also pull cash out of your motorcycle, boat, motor home, or trailer—in fact, anything that you can talk your bank into loaning money against! It works the same way as refinancing your car.

How Much You Can Raise

Anywhere between 75 and 100 percent of the wholesale value of your car; usually $1,500 to $10,000.

How Fast

Auto loans can be set up in three to five business days.

Credit Needed

You generally need good credit in order to obtain a used-car loan.

Advantages

Approval is very easy. Most banks are happy to make auto loans because the loan is secured by something tangible that they can sell quickly if they ever have to repossess it. Banks have a pretty good success rate on auto "paper," and they make good profits on it. Just about any financial institution offers auto loans, so you don't have to waste much time searching around. You can do most of your shopping and comparing rates over the phone. Your loan should be all wrapped up in just a couple of days.

Disadvantages

Interest rates on used-car loans can be pretty high (15 to 22 percent). This may be a lot higher than other loans you could obtain. Also, if you get behind on your payments, the lender can repossess your car. Not only does this leave you without a ride, it leaves a large blot on your credit rating.

#16. Draw Out Your Company Pension or Savings Plan

If you have worked at a company for several years, you may have built up a pension or savings plan that is quite substantial. In many instances, you can draw this money out if you need it. Talk to your company's benefits administrator, controller, or office manager. He or she can give you the details on this kind of withdrawal.

Your pension money is there to help you when you retire, in addition to your Social Security and other benefits. If you do draw out this money, be sure to use it for a wise investment, such as a buying a home or rental property, or starting a business. Use the money for something that will provide you with some income or other security later on. Don't use it foolishly. It may have taken you years to put it away.

There may also be some tax consequences if this money has accrued tax deferred. Talk to a knowledgeable accountant. If you have to pay a large tax penalty, you may decide that there are other, cheaper ways to come up with money than this.

One thing that can be said for using your pension money now is that if you use it, you'll never lose it. What if your company goes bankrupt, taking its pension plan with it? There is pension insurance for this type of emergency, but it can't always be relied upon. There's nothing more devastating than to work all your life planning to retire on your company pension, only to see the company fail and your entire pension disappear. If you have any doubts about the fiscal security of your company, you might want to take your pension money and run!

How Much You Can Raise

You can raise as much as you have built up in your company pension or savings plan.

How Fast

Dispersments from this type of account can take several weeks and may have to come from the main office in some other state.

Credit Needed

Your credit rating doesn't matter since you are not applying for a loan.

Advantages

You may have built up a large nest egg, which is yours to use in any way you wish. It may be a better idea to use this money than to borrow money elsewhere. Also, by spending your pension money now, you are insuring that you will be able to use it, rather than waiting until you retire and possibly losing it all through business bankruptcy.

Disadvantages

You are using money that is intended to help you financially when you retire. Use the money for some income-producing investment, such as real estate or a business. Also, there may be tax consequences of drawing out your pension money early.

#17. Have Tenants Prepay Rent

If you own rental property, you may be able to collect extra money fast by having your tenants prepay their rents. Here's how this works.

First, send a letter to all of your tenants stating that if they will prepay the next year's rent or lease payment, you will give them a discount of 5 or 10 percent and will not raise their rent during that period. So if their rent is $400, offer to let them pay $4,300 to $4,500 up front, instead of $4,800 on a month-to-month basis. Of course, this presupposes that your tenants have the ability to pay, or borrow, that kind of money. You should also check to see if there are any state or local laws that would govern or restrict this type of transaction.

The advantage to the tenants is clear. They will save 5 to 10 percent of their annual rent payments if they can afford to pay you the full amount up front. As a bonus, by paying for a year's rent in advance, they lock out any rent increase. This is great for a tenant who likes living in your property and plans to stay for an extended period anyway.

Let's take this idea a step further. Let's assume that you have ten tenants who pay an average rent of $400. If only half of the tenants take you up on your offer, you could raise about $22,000! Quite a substantial sum.

WARNING

If you use this method to raise cash, by all means invest the money in some investment that will produce at least enough income to replace the rents you will be losing. Otherwise, you may have a very tough time making your own mortgage payments.

HOW MUCH YOU CAN RAISE

This depends on your total rents and how many of your tenants are willing to take you up on the offer. This plan saves tenants a lot of money, but they may not have the funds on hand to take advantage of it. As you see by the example above, it's possible to raise a very large amount of money this way.

HOW FAST

You usually need to give your tenants about thirty days' notice for this type of offer. This will give them time to raise the funds necessary.

CREDIT NEEDED

Your credit rating doesn't matter.

ADVANTAGES

You are simply getting an advance on money that would eventually come to you anyway. No lending institutions are involved, no credit checks, no red tape. You have complete control over the way the money is spent. If your properties have large positive cash flows, you may not even miss the monthly rent payments.

DISADVANTAGES

The main disadvantage is that you are using money that

has not yet been earned. This could get you into trouble if you can't pay your current mortgage, tax, or utility bills down the road. To avoid this, don't use this type of fund-raising unless you use the proceeds in a real estate investment or other business that will produce the cash flow that you will be missing.

#18. Collect Increased Security Deposits

If you own a few rental units, you may be able to raise some extra cash by collecting increased security deposits. Let's assume that you own five units and that the average rent on each is $350. It is customary for your last month rent/security deposit to be at least as much as the rent itself. Therefore, if your monthly rents are $1,750, you should have at least that amount in security deposits.

If you don't have any security deposits, or if they are a very small amount per unit, you may want to increase them. Below is a sample letter that you can use for this purpose. When I send this letter to tenants, I make it plain that this is only a security deposit, not a rent increase. I also give the renter the option to pay the increase up front or in small monthly payments of $25 or $50. I also write that the entire security deposit (or any amount that you feel is reasonable) will be refunded when the tenant moves out as long as all rents are current and the unit is in good shape.

Dear Tenant,

At the time our company bought this property, your existing security deposit was only $50. Our policy is that all security deposits have to equal at least one month's rent. Since your rent is $400 per month, we will need to keep on file an additional $350. This amount may be paid all at once on the first of next month, or you may pay it in payments of $50 per month.

Of course, this money is only held by our company for security and will be refunded in full when you decide to move (as long as your apartment is clean and in satisfactory condition). Thank you for your cooperation in this matter.

I have used this letter almost a dozen times and have never had any problems with the tenants. Still be sure and check to see if there are any state or local laws or regulations governing the collection and use of security deposit funds.

How Much You Can Raise
This depends on how large your entire rent roll is and how much you have already collected in the past. You can usually get security deposits that equal your entire monthly rent.

How Fast
You generally have to give your tenants a thirty-day notice whenever there is a change in your rental policy or amounts. Most tenants will opt for the small monthly payment rather than coming up with a large lump sum, but even then you will have a substantial monthly increase in amount of rent you are receiving.

Credit Needed
Your credit rating doesn't matter.

ADVANTAGES

There are several advantages to raising money from increased security deposits on your rentals. One is that this money is like an interest-free loan (although in some states, you have to pay your renters nominal interest on their security deposits). Another is that you don't have to pay this money back until your tenant decides to move out. One last thought: Regardless of whether you collect security deposits to raise cash, it's always a very good idea to have them. They protect you, the owner, against losses due to property damage and unpaid rents. Also, having some of the tenants' money on file tends to make them more responsible with your property.

DISADVANTAGES

It's difficult to raise large sums of cash with this method. You are limited to your current rents, to how many units you have, and to what the market will bear. But the main disadvantage is that the money you raise actually belongs to the tenants, and you will have to return it when they move out (as long as their rent is current and they leave the property in good shape). The problem is that they may move out when you have the money tied up somewhere. Security deposits are like small loans that can be called due at any time, whether or not it is convenient to you. Also, if your lease specifies the amount of the security deposit the tenant must pay, you cannot increase that amount without your tenant's permission.

#19. FHA Title 1 Home Loan

An FHA (Federal Housing Administration) Title 1 home loan is a home-improvement loan that is insured by the federal government. Most commercial lenders offer the Title 1, and since it is insured by the government, it is surprisingly easy to get. The maximum loan amount is $17,500 on a single family house, and the repayment period is usually ten to fifteen years.

The government came up with the Title 1 loan to help homeowners and landlords refurbish their property. The unique feature about the loan is that you don't have to have any equity in your property in order to qualify for it. This can come in very handy if you have just purchased a property and need to get a loan but don't yet have much equity.

To find out about a Title 1 loan, call your local commercial bank and ask if it is familiar with this type of loan program. Some lenders may not be. Another place to look is in the real estate classified ads. Look for ads that mention "$17,500" or "no equity required." These are the key points of the Title 1 loan.

After you have filled out an application, the lender will check your credit, income, and employment information to make sure you have the means to pay back the loan. As I mentioned above, because the loan is government backed, the lender is not taking much of a risk, and the loan is very easy to qualify for. The lender will send an appraiser out to look at the property, but again, this is mostly a formality as there is no equity required to back the loan.

The lender will also need a detailed list of the improvements you plan to make with the loan proceeds. Be sure to get estimates from painters, roofers, and contractors. You can do some or all of the improvements yourself, but you will still need to fill out a complete plan of the renovations and their material costs. The lender will call you about six months after making the loan in order to send over an appraiser to verify that the proposed renovations that you listed on your application have been completed. Most lenders charge from two to ten points to set up a Title 1 loan. Generally, the higher the interest rate, the fewer the points, and vice versa. On the full $17,500 loan, the fee can range anywhere from $400 to $1,800. This is quite high, but then again, no one else will lend you money on a house if you have no equity. The maximum loan amortized over fifteen years will cost only about $235 per month, which is not too bad!

After the deal is approved and you have signed all the papers, you will have to wait three days before you get your money. This is the legally required "cooling off" period you have to back out of any real estate loan.

How Much You Can Raise

The maximum you can raise is $17,500. After points and other costs, you should net $16,000 to $17,000.

How Fast

Figure on about three weeks from start to finish.

Credit Needed

Since you are dealing with normal commercial lenders, you need a relatively good credit rating to qualify for this type of loan.

Advantages

No equity is required. The maximum amount—$17,500—is high. The loan is very easy to qualify for. You can do some or all of the renovations yourself—the work doesn't have to be done by a contractor. So in essence you can "pay yourself." Approval time is relatively quick, and it doesn't matter how many existing liens you already have on the property.

Disadvantages

The points and loan costs are very high—up to 10 percent. This makes a Title 1 loan an expensive way to borrow. Also, the loan requirements limit your freedom to use the proceeds in any way you wish. The money is supposed to be used for property renovation, not a new car or a Mexican vacation. Some people do use the money for other things, but this was not the original intent of the government when this program was set up.

#20. Borrow from Your Real Estate Agent ·

When you purchase a piece of property, several other people have as much interest as you do in seeing that the deal closes. Think about it for a moment. There is the selling agent, who will earn a commission; the buyer's agent, who will earn a commission; and the seller himself. All three of these people have a vested interest in closing that sale. You can use that interest to your advantage.

Buying and selling agents each usually earn 2 to 3 percent of the selling price of a property. So if you are buying a house or rental property for, let's say, $150,000, both the buyer's agent and the seller's agent will earn commissions of between $3,000 and $4,500. (If the agent works for a real estate broker, the agent usually receives 2 percent and the broker receives 1 percent.) They will receive this money at the close of the escrow.

If you happen to be a few thousand dollars short on your

down payment, you may be able to borrow this money from the agent. Here's how it works. Let's assume you need $12,000 to close the deal, but after scraping up all the money you can, you are still $3,000 short. If the agent is getting at least this much commission on the sale, he may be willing to lend the money to you to help you close the deal, and secure his or her loan to you with a second trust deed against the property. Since you are dealing with a real estate sales person and not a lending institution, you can work out just about any terms and repayment schedules that you can agree on. Agents are generally willing to go along with this type of plan because they will close a sale and earn a commission, even if they can't receive it all now. And if there is one thing that real estate agents like to have backing their loans, it's real estate. The entire transaction can be drawn up by the escrow company as part of the normal closing on the property.

How Much You Can Raise

The agent will earn 2 to 3 percent of the selling price of the property. You may be able to borrow at least that amount, and there is nothing that says you cannot work the same type of deal with the seller's agent and borrow another 2 or 3 percent. Or if the selling agent is also the listing agent, he or she may be willing to loan their entire 4 to 6 percent commission.

How Fast

This is generally handled at the close of escrow, although it is a wise idea to work out the details long before the closing day. Your agent will probably not appreciate it if you spring this on him at the last moment.

Credit Needed

If your credit is really poor, you may not be able to get a new home loan in the first place. Your credit and income will have to be pretty good or else the real estate agent may not be willing to loan you his or her commission to help close the deal.

ADVANTAGES

This is an excellent way to raise money for your real estate purchases. Everyone wins: The seller sells the property, the agents earn a commission (although they will not receive it for a while), and you get a small loan without having to go through a bank or other financial institution. You also get to purchase a piece of real estate that otherwise would have been out of your reach. Since you are dealing with an individual and not a bank, you can work out any terms you can both agree upon. You may want to make no payments for a year, or no payments at all (just the full amount plus interest due on a certain date—a "balloon" payment). You can negotiate any interest rate you want, or you may pay no interest at all. It's up to you!

DISADVANTAGES

About the only disadvantage to borrowing your agent's commission to help with your down payment is that he will probably secure his loan with a second trust deed on the property. This means that if you ever get behind with your payments, the agent has the legal right to start foreclosure proceedings and possibly take over your property. Also, with a second trust deed already on the property, you may be hampered in securing additional financing for your property. Each succeeding lender is assigned a lower priority in recovering his money in case of a default (hence first trust deed, second trust deed, and so on). Not many lenders like to be third or fourth in line.

#21. Borrow from Friends and Relatives

One of the easiest ways to get cash fast is to simply borrow it from your friends and relatives. As a matter of fact, this is probably how most people raise cash for major purchases and business opportunities. You might even get the loan interest-free!

It is a good idea to have an attorney draw up some kind of loan papers if you are borrowing a substantial amount. This can save a lot of hassles later on.

HOW MUCH YOU CAN RAISE

With friends and family, the sky's the limit! You can borrow as much as they can afford and are willing to part with.

HOW FAST

The process is about as fast as it takes to make out a check.

CREDIT NEEDED

Your friends and family are not going to judge your creditworthiness as harshly as a bank would, so your past credit may not be a big factor. Friends and family can be pretty forgiving.

ADVANTAGES

There are myriad reasons to borrow from friends and family instead of from a bank or other lending institution. They are:

- If you can convince them that your idea is sound, there is no limit (within their means) as to how much you can borrow from them. Family and friends probably don't have preset lending criteria.
- You can borrow the money quickly and with a minimum of hassle.
- You can use the money for anything you choose, with no strings attached from the lender.
- You can probably borrow regardless of your past credit rating.
- You can work out just about any repayment schedule that you choose.

DISADVANTAGES

There are two main disadvantages to borrowing from friends and relatives. First, when you borrow money from a relative, they may want to butt into your life and give you advice that you don't want and didn't ask for. They may think that they can control you because you owe them money. Second, if—God forbid—your business or investment were to fail, you would have to live with the embarrassment of defaulting on a loan from your own family. You'd think about it every time you got together. You can avoid seeing your local banker a lot more easily than you can avoid seeing your friends or relatives. You could even lose good friendships or contact with close relatives because you don't want to be reminded of the money you owe them.

#22. "Help Ad" in the Newspaper

If you have exhausted all the traditional ways to raise cash without success, you may want to try putting an ad in the newspaper asking for help. Several publications carry this type of advertising; you can find anything from tiny ads in *The National Enquirer*, to large-column ads in the business section of the *Los Angeles Times* and *The Wall Street Journal*.

Depending on how much money you can afford for the advertising, there are several ways to set up your money request. If you can spare only a few dollars, you might try a small ad requesting a loan, with your name and address, so that people with money to lend can contact you. When they respond to your ad, send them back a letter explaining why you need the loan and how and when you intend to pay it back. Work out the details ahead of time. The more organized you are, the better your request will be received. By that, I mean figure out how much you need, what the funds will be used for, what payment schedule you will use to repay the loan, and what interest rate you will pay.

Don't expect someone to just give you money—there is no Santa Claus. Be reasonable in your expectations. Someone may be willing to loan you the money if your request makes sense.

If you are looking for a large amount of money for purchasing real estate or starting a business, it's better to place a large ad in the business section of a large metropolitan newspaper. You can find these ads every day. They often look something like this:

Needed $50,000 for purchasing 4 unit rental property. Loan secured by 2nd on property. Will pay 13%, due in 3 years. Call 555-1234.

The ad states the amount needed, for what purpose, at what interest rate, for how long, and the security offered— just about everything a potential lender would initially need to know.

When lenders begin to call, it is a good idea to have a fact sheet ready by the phone with all the pertinent information. Again, the better prepared and more professional you appear, the better chance you have of getting a loan. The people that call will generally not be conventional lenders. They will be private individuals with money to invest. They will be loaning out their hard-earned money on your word alone, so do everything in your power to appear professional, trustworthy, and prepared.

How Much You Can Raise

Technically, you could raise hundreds of thousands of dollars by using "help ads" in the newspapers. Generally, though, smaller amounts are more practical for this type of lending.

How Fast

Generally, ads have to be placed a month or two before a magazine or national tabloid's publication date (with local newspapers, the lead time may be as little as one or two days). After your ad is published, it may be a couple of weeks before you get any responses, then a couple more weeks of correspondence or phone calls back and forth before you obtain any money. Faster ways are certainly available to raise cash.

Credit Needed

This may be a good way to raise cash if you have poor credit and cannot get money from a more traditional lender. If you have good credit, use that to your advantage. You may even show your credit report to potential lenders to build your credibility.

Advantages

Since you are not using a conventional lender, you may be able to obtain funds for some very unconventional purposes. The purpose for which you use the money is up to you, as long as you can get an investor to go along with your plans and ideas. Since you are arranging the loan with a private individual, the term and interest rate will be whatever you can negotiate. Also, you may be able to get several people to invest in the same idea, enabling you to raise even more cash.

Disadvantages

Obviously, you may not be able to find anyone to loan you money in this manner. You are simply placing an ad, hoping to find potential lenders and investors. It may or may not work, but then, you probably wouldn't try this way unless you had already been turned down several times by more conventional lenders. Also, this type of loan may take three to four months to set up, so it won't be much help if you need the money fast. Finally, there may be legal fees involved because you should ask an attorney to draw up the necessary paperwork for you.

#23. Bill Consolidation Loan

You are buried under a mountain of bills and are not making enough money to catch up. Each month you simply fall further and further behind. One way you might raise cash is through a "bill consolidation loan." Most banks offer this kind of loan: It allows you to pay off all your current bills and make just one monthly payment that's lower than the combined monthly payments on all the other bills.

Let's say you are paying the following monthly payments with these balances:

Creditor	Monthly Payment	Balance
Sears	$ 35	$ 680
Penney's	$ 50	$ 850
VISA	$ 80	$ 600
MasterCard	$ 75	$ 550

Car payment	$165	$1,350
Local bank	$105	$ 850
Furniture store	$ 90	$ 480
Total Debt	$600	$5,360

As you can see, it is costing you $600 per month to service a debt of only $5,360. (This example is used as an illustration only—your actual debts and payments may be much higher.) In the example, most of the payments are short-term or revolving credit. This means that a substantial portion is required each month for debt service. By getting a bill consolidation loan of $5,400 for thirty-six months at 13 percent, the total monthly payment would come to only about $181. You could pay off all your current bills in full—and save almost $420 per month! A bill consolidation loan stretches out your payments. You pay a lot less each month for a longer period of time. This type of loan can give you some breathing room and allow you to keep your good credit.

Most lenders offer a bill consolidation loan of one sort or another. Some collateral is usually required.

How Much You Can Raise

If you have collateral to back up the loan, you may be able to borrow up to $50,000 or more.

How Fast

A bill consolidation loan usually requires about a week to process.

Credit Needed

You generally need good credit, although some companies cater to less creditworthy borrowers. Look for them in the telephone directory under "Loans."

Advantages

There are several advantages. First of all, you can pay off all your current creditors in full, ahead of time. This will show up very well on your credit rating. Second, your new monthly payment may be substantially lower than what you are now paying. Third, by getting your loans paid off, you achieve a little piece of mind—no bill collectors hounding you! And you can use the extra money you save every month to start building up a savings or investment program.

DISADVANTAGES

Generally, you are going to end up paying more interest in the long run because you are stretching your loan out for a longer period of time. This happens even though the bill consolidation loan you set up has a lower interest rate than several of your current credit cards and loans. Also, by the time you decide to apply for a bill consolidation loan, you may already be behind on several of your current loans. Remember, apply for this type of loan at the time when you see that you may be getting behind on your bills in the future. Don't wait until you are several months late to apply for this type of loan. That may make it much more difficult to qualify, and you may have to pay a much higher rate of interest.

Another disadvantage of this type of loan is that once you have your old bills paid off, you may be tempted to run out, buy more junk and run up your balances all over again. Don't do it. Use the extra money every month to begin a savings program or some other worthwhile investment.

#24. Take a Salary Advance

What would your boss say if you walked in and asked for a $2,000 salary advance? Give it a try—you may be happy with the results!

All of us run into a money crunch every now and then. Your employer understands this and may be willing to help out with a short-term salary advance. Unfortunately, most of us are too afraid to ask for it. Put yourself in your boss's shoes. If you had a very reliable and trustworthy employee that needed a few thousand dollars for some emergency, wouldn't you lend him or her a hand? It's not a handout—all you are asking is to be paid a couple of weeks or months ahead of time. When you think about it, it doesn't seem like such a tremendous request, does it?

Before you approach your employer, work out a detailed plan showing what the money will be used for, how you could pay it back if that becomes necessary, and how you will be able to survive on a reduced paycheck for the near future. Don't walk into his office groveling. Approach your employer as a fellow businessperson who happens to be in need of a short-term cash infusion. You are a good risk. He writes your paycheck. Who has more control over your money? Who has a better chance of being paid back?

How Much You Can Raise

This depends upon your normal salary. An employer can usually be persuaded to advance a reliable employee about one month's wages.

How Fast

As fast as your employer can write a check.

Credit Needed

Your previous credit should not be a big factor, although if your credit is excellent, you should certainly bring that up in your proposal.

Advantages

You are raising funds without borrowing, which is always a good idea. There will probably not be any interest or other costs involved. The time frame to get the funds is very quick. And finally, on an intangible level, it's nice for your self-esteem to know that your boss trusts you enough to advance your salary.

Disadvantages

There are many disadvantages. First of all, you don't ever want to become a "problem" to your organization. You always want to give more to your company than you take. You don't want to use up too many favors. Your employer sees you as an asset to the company. If you become a liability (by making too many special requests), you may no longer have a job. Second, using the advance money to pay off the current crisis, may leave you with nothing to pay the bills next month. Third, for some unforeseen circumstance, you may lose your job—how will you pay the money back?

A salary advance "loan" may not be right for everybody. It takes careful planning (next month's budget) and the right atmosphere at your job. But it's a quick way to raise cash in an emergency.

#25. Sell Future Commissions

Selling future commissions is very common in the real estate sales industry. An agent earns commissions that will not be paid for several weeks or months, for one reason or another. Rather than waiting for this money to be paid, the agent sells the commissions to his or her broker for a slight discount.

If you happen to be in the sales field and have earned commissions that will not be paid for some time, you may be able to use this idea. I know that this type of plan works in real estate, automobile, and some other types of sales occupations. Approach your supervisors and try to work out some kind of prepayment on commissions that you have already earned. In most cases, you will not even have to discount the amount that is due to you. Give it a try. You certainly have nothing to lose.

How Much You Can Raise

This depends on how much you have coming to you in future commissions.

How Fast

Generally, you can receive the money during the next pay period.

Credit Needed

Your credit rating doesn't matter.

Advantages

This is a good way to raise cash without having to borrow. The money would be yours eventually—you are just trying to receive it a little sooner than it would normally come. After all, why should you let your company float you on commissions? Better for the money to be in your account earning interest than in your company's.

Disadvantages

Be careful with this plan. Make sure that you are not counting your chickens before they hatch. By that, I mean that you shouldn't obtain and use the money now if there is any chance that your sale could fall through and you could owe the money to your employer. Also, it's always a good idea to build up some kind of savings. These future commissions held by your employer could serve that purpose. Finally, if you have to discount the amount owed to you in order to receive it immediately, there may be cheaper ways to raise the cash you need.

#26. Student Loan

If you need money for college, dozens of excellent loan programs are available, from both the state governments and the federal government. These education loans can be used for any purpose having to do with your education; tuition, books, lab fees, living costs while at school, and so on.

To give you some idea of the tremendous amounts of money available through education loans, we'll look at just one program—Perkins loans. Perkins loans are a federal loan program that is available to students needing financial assistance. You may borrow up to $9,000 to help you work toward your bachelor's degree. The interest rate is only 5 percent, and the repayment doesn't start until you have been out of school for at least nine months. Depending on the size of the loan, students have up to ten years to repay. Not a bad program! And there are several other plans just like this one.

To find out more about these various loan programs, contact the financial aid officers at your local college or university. They can tell you what student loan programs you qualify for and how to apply for them.

How Much You Can Raise

Some student loan programs come to as much as $50,000 or more over the course of your education. This money is usually given to you in increments as your schooling progresses, rather than all up front.

How Fast

It usually takes a month or two from the time you initially apply until you have the money in your hands.

Credit Needed

The nice thing about student loans is that good credit is usually not necessary. As a matter of fact, since most people who apply for student loans are relatively young, many of them have never qualified for any other type of credit before!

Advantages

There are several advantages to using student loans to finance your education. First, you may be able to attend a better college or pursue a more extensive education since the extra money is available. Second, the terms on most student loans are fantastic! The interest rates are generally low, the repayment periods long, and your monthly payments don't start until after you have graduated.

Disadvantages

First, if you come from an affluent family, you may not qualify for a student loan because the financial hardship is not there. Next, you don't get all the money up front but doled out piecemeal as you continue your education. Finally, even if you don't graduate, the loan has to be repaid. This may cause financial hardship if you have dropped out of college without getting your degree.

#27. Education Grant

If you are interested in going to college but can't afford it or don't qualify for any of the education loan programs available, you may want to look into education grants. A grant is money given free to students who meet certain qualifications (such as pursuing particular courses of study or belonging to particular ethnic or religious groups). The government and private groups and businesses give out education grants, and they can be used in just about any field of learning, including trade schools. The amazing thing is that many of these grants are never used!

These grants are given out by organizations trying to promote education in certain fields. Their amounts range anywhere from $500 to more than $50,000! The money can be used for tuition, books, and general living expenses having to do with your college education.

To find out more about education grants, you can look in your library's reference section. There is usually an entire section on scholarships and grants. Some excellent books on the subject are: *Free Money For College* and *Free Money for Graduate Studies*, both by Laurie Blum, and the most recent edition of *The College Blue Book—Scholarships, Fellowships, Grants and Loans*.

HOW MUCH YOU CAN RAISE

You can raise anywhere from $500 to $50,000 or more.

HOW FAST

You can go through the various steps to acquire an education grant in about two months.

CREDIT NEEDED

Your credit is not a factor since the money doesn't have to be paid back.

ADVANTAGES

There are many advantages to using education grants. First and most important, the money never has to be repaid. This is the difference between a grant and a loan. If your field of learning qualifies you for a single grant or several, by all means, take advantage of them! This extra money may allow you to enter a better college or university, or to complete an education, even when you are out of funds from other sources.

DISADVANTAGES

The primary disadvantage of education grants is that none may be available for your particular field of endeavor, or none at the time you need one (although there are so many types of grants, just about anyone qualifies for one of them!) Also, large grants generally come in increments as your education progresses, not in a lump sum. Another disadvantage with grants is that you have to compete for them with other deserving students, and the competition may be fierce.

#28. Rent or Lease Your Next Major Purchase

If you need money in order to buy a car, computer, airplane, boat, or just about any other major item, why not try renting or leasing it in order to save you cash?

These days, companies offer to rent or lease just about any item you could possibly desire. The major difference between renting and leasing is that leasing normally locks you into a longer, scheduled period, while you can rent most items on a monthly, weekly, or even daily basis. By renting or leasing instead of buying outright, you:

- conserve your capital (less initial outlay means a better cash flow);
- get a chance to try out a product to see if it works for you;
- save on repair and maintenance costs (which are usually handled by the rental or leasing company);
- don't get locked into an older model and may be

able to change and upgrade the equipment on a regular basis;

- get a lot better product than you could afford if you were paying cash;

- may be able to work out a plan in which part of your monthly payment goes toward the principal if you eventually decide to buy the item; and

- possibly get a better tax deduction.

Given all this, it often makes sense to lease or rent a major item rather than to scrounge up the cash to pay for it. Keep your cash for more important things and look into renting or leasing the next time you need to buy a major item.

How Much You Can Raise

If you qualify, you can rent or lease just about anything, with values up to hundreds of thousands of dollars.

How Fast

These rentals and leases come through usually within a day or two.

Credit Needed

You generally need very good credit in order to lease or buy major items.

Advantages

When you rent or lease, you get a chance to try the product out to see if it's right for you, without shelling out the entire purchase price. This allows you to conserve capital and in many cases to afford a much better product than if you had to buy it outright. By renting or leasing, you are generally spared the costs of repairs and maintenance.

Disadvantages

The main disadvantage with renting or leasing is that you end up paying a lot more for an item than you would have if you had bought it outright to begin with. You build up no equity. The entire payment goes toward rental, interest, and general carrying costs—none toward the principal balance (unless otherwise negotiated).

#29. Sale/Leaseback

If you own a home, paid for or not, or a business with a lot of high-priced equipment (such as computers or other machines), you may be able to raise money through what's called a sale/leaseback. Airlines and other cash-starved businesses have been doing this for years.

Here's how it works: Let's say that TWA needs to raise some quick cash. It can sell one of its 747s to a leasing company for, say, $50 million. Then it can lease the same airplane back from the leasing company for $500,000 per month. TWA still gets full use of the aircraft, but it also gets a $50 million cash injection. The leasing company borrows the $50 million from a bank using the 747 as collateral. The leasing company pays TWA the $50 million and then uses the lease payments from TWA to pay back the loan and hopefully make a profit. If TWA can't make the lease payments, the leasing company can repossess the 747 in order to pay off the loan. The deal works for all parties involved.

That's great for TWA, you may be thinking, but how can you use the same concept to raise cash? Well, if you own a home (whether it is completely paid for or not), you may be able to sell it to an investor and lease it back from him on a long-term basis. You get all your cash now, and you can still remain in your home (as long as you make your lease payments). The lease payments may even be lower than your current mortgage, because you are not building any equity in the property. You may also be able to add a clause to the lease contract allowing you to buy the home back for a set price once you are back on your feet financially.

The investor in this deal gets a nice clean rental property with a long-term tenant who will take good care of the property. Talk to your real estate broker. He or she will probably know several investors who are interested in this sort of arrangement. You might also want to put an ad in the paper describing this type of arrangement. It shouldn't be too hard to find investors interested in this plan.

If you own a business with expensive equipment, you can sell the equipment to a leasing company and then lease it back. It works the same as the TWA example above. Just look in the Yellow Pages under "Leasing Companies." In any major city there are several who do this kind of a sale/leaseback every day.

How Much You Can Raise

This depends on how much equity you have in your home, or how much your business equipment is worth.

How Fast

For a home, it may take four to eight months to find an interested investor and complete the sale and escrow. For business machines or equipment, you can probably complete the transaction in two or three weeks.

CREDIT NEEDED

If you are using your home, your credit is unimportant since you are simply cashing out. For business equipment, your good credit is very important since the lease terms will be partially based on your previous credit history. The better your credit, the better the terms you will be able to negotiate. If your credit is terrible, you may not be able to use this business plan at all.

Note that when you sell your home, you are required (in most cases) to pay taxes on the profit. Check with your tax preparer or accountant for details regarding your situation.

ADVANTAGES

If you are in financial trouble and may lose your home, it makes a lot of sense to sell it to an investor who will lease it back to you on a long-term basis. This way, you can cash out and keep all your equity and still stay in your home. You don't have to face the trauma of foreclosure. You don't even have to move. You may even be able to cut your monthly outgo if you can negotiate a lease payment that is lower than your current mortgage payment. If you are using the sale/leaseback in your business, you free up a lot of capital that can be used for other purposes.

DISADVANTAGES

When you sell your home, you obviously no longer get the tax savings and equity-building benefits that are available to owners. You are now, in effect, renting a home. For a business, the only drawback may be the added costs involved in leasing equipment that you now own outright—although the lump sum in cash you will receive may make up for this.

#30. Skip Your Payments

Maybe you need a large amount of cash quickly, or maybe it's bill-paying time and you're broke, or maybe you need money for other purposes. If so, you may be able to skip most of your payments for one month! Here's how:

First, contact each of your creditors: the savings and loan that carries your mortgage, the bank that has you car loans, your credit card companies, and the others. Contact the credit manager, and explain to him or her that things are a little tight this month. Ask if it would be okay if you skipped your payment for this one month, or perhaps paid interest only. Tell the manager that you understand the importance of good credit, and you don't want this one time extension to give your credit a black eye. You simply need a little breathing room. Most of your creditors will go along with this idea—as long as you contact them *in advance!* Don't ever just skip a payment and wait for your creditors to call you. Set up the whole plan ahead of time.

It is a good idea to send each credit manager a letter confirming your agreement in writing. Keep a copy for your records.

Your mortgage holder will probably need at least an interest-only payment from you. Your credit card companies will probably ask for the same thing. The bank that has your auto loan will probably let you skip a payment (and just add it on to the end of your loan) as long as you haven't been late in the past and are current with your payments now. Most of the smaller creditors you owe (businesses and small department stores), generally have the leeway to allow you to skip one payment completely if they choose to. All you have to do is call and ask.

Remember: This plan works only if you are currently paying your bills on time. If you are constantly late with your payments, your creditors are much less likely to allow you a one-month grace period. Also, be sure to set this all up ahead of time. Don't just skip your payments and wait for the lenders to call you!

How Much You Can Raise

You could conceivably raise as much money as you pay out in a month to creditors. For example, if all your debt payments total $1,500 each month and you get all your creditors to give you a one-month extension, you can save the entire $1,500 to keep or spend on other things.

How Fast

You can arrange the entire plan in just a week or two.

Credit Needed

If you are constantly late on your payments, it's unlikely that any lender would grant you a credit extension.

Advantages

If you have nowhere else to turn, this may be a good way to save some big money in a hurry. Or if you see that you are going to get behind in your bills, this is a good plan to give you a month of breathing room with very little hassle from your creditors.

DISADVANTAGES

By using this plan, you are simply postponing paying your bills, not paying them off. Some of your creditors may not want to grant you any extension or grace period, which defeats the whole program. Also, you will end up paying more interest because of the postponement.

#31. SBA Loan

The Small Business Administration (SBA) is a government agency set up to help small business grow and prosper. It offers all kinds of services to the small business owner, the most important of which is business loans. If you own a small business (and 95 percent of all companies in this country are considered small businesses by SBA standards) or are considering starting one, the SBA is a good place to go to raise some cash.

The SBA makes two kinds of loans—guaranteed and direct. Guaranteed loans are made by banks and backed by the SBA. Direct loans are made by the SBA itself. Such loans are available for just about any small business use: for startup costs, inventory, equipment, machinery, land, or buildings. The amounts available, the interest rates, and the terms vary according to the purpose of the loan. Before you can apply for an SBA loan, you have to be turned down for a business loan by a regular financial institution.

You can get further information on SBA loans by calling the Small Business Administration listed under "U.S. Government" in your phone book. Your local SBA office will be happy to send you all the information you need to apply for a small business loan.

When you apply for an SBA loan, you are competing with other small business owners for a limited pool of funds. The size of that pool varies each year with congressional appropriations. To have a better shot at getting a loan, you may want to get help in preparing your loan package. There are companies that will help you prepare a loan package for a fee. They can be found advertised in the business section of most major metropolitan newspapers. Or you may want to contact SCORE (Service Corps of Retired Executives). This organization consists of retired businessmen who freely donate their time and talents to help build small business. You can find your local SCORE chapter in the Yellow Pages.

How Much You Can Raise

You can raise as much as several hundred thousand dollars, if your business plan and assets warrant it.

How Fast

It takes about a month, since the loan package is so involved.

Credit Needed

The SBA is not going to loan thousands of dollars to someone with poor credit and a half-baked business proposal. Good credit and a good business plan are very important, since you are in competition with many other entrepreneurs for the same money.

Advantages

The SBA is kind of the lender of last resort for aspiring small businessmen and women. It will often make startup loans that a regular bank wouldn't touch. Also, SBA loans are usually at a lower interest rate and have longer terms than conventional bank loans, which lowers your repayment costs.

DISADVANTAGES

The major disadvantage of SBA loans is that they are not easy to get. Since you have to compete with other small business owners, your loan package and business plan have to be outstanding. Also, since you are dealing with a government bureaucracy, your paperwork and required reports are extensive and very time-consuming.

#32. Barter

Depending upon why you need to raise money, you may be able to use barter instead. Barter is simply the exchange of your goods or services for something else of value, without using any cash.

Here's how to go about it. Let's say that you need to raise money to buy a new $5,000 boat. Approach the seller and ask if there is anything he needs or wants, instead of cash, in exchange for the boat. Is he selling the boat in order to raise money for something else that he needs? If you can somehow meet this need, no cash has to be transferred between you. For example, if the seller of the boat actually needs to raise the money to landscape his house or put a new roof on it, perhaps you can provide these services for him. No cash actually has to change hands. You get the boat, and the seller gets his landscaping or a new roof or whatever else you have decided upon.

Make sure that the service you agree to perform is something that you can handle or that you know of someone who can help you with it. That way, you won't get halfway through and realize that you can't finish the job or that the quality is not up to the seller's standards.

The key to bartering is to be creative. Ask the other person questions. Get to know him a little. What can you do to fulfill his needs in order to get the products or services that you desire?

Many products available by swap or barter are listed in the classified section of your local newspaper. There may even be barter clubs and organizations in your area. Look in the Yellow Pages under "Barter." With these clubs, you may be able to swap a few hours of labor in your particular specialty in trade for other products and services. You build up credits, which are computerized and matched up with others who use your service.

HOW MUCH YOU CAN RAISE

Barter does have its limits. You have to offer something of equal value to the seller of the product or service you want. If the barter just involves your labor, think about how long you will have to work in order to earn the item that you want.

HOW FAST

It takes as long as you need to talk the other person into swapping or bartering his product for yours, to complete the transaction.

CREDIT NEEDED

Since no loan is involved, a good credit rating is not necessary.

ADVANTAGES

One advantage is that since you barter for an item, no cash has to change hands. You don't have to borrow money, or even earn it and pay taxes on it. And since you don't actually exchange any money, you may be able to get some very good deals, because what may be of little value to you could be very valuable to someone else. Even nations often barter their goods and services for the products of other countries.

DISADVANTAGES

It may be difficult to find someone who is willing to exchange something that they want to sell for your goods or services. They may prefer to get cash instead. The key to barter is to find someone who is willing to go along with it. Apart from that, there are no major drawbacks with the barter system.

#33. Sweat Equity

If you are trying to raise money to make a down payment on a rental property or to purchase a business, you may want to try "sweat equity." Sweat equity simply means using your muscles, sweat, and labor instead of your cash.

Let's say that you and your prospective partner have found a home or rental property that you would like to purchase, but you are short on cash. You can make a deal with your prospective partner that, if he'll come up with the majority of the down payment, you will work on the property on your free time for a certain number of hours instead of coming up with any money. For example, you might strike a deal in which your partner comes up with the $5,000 down payment you need to buy the property. For your share of the down payment, you agree to do work on the property, such as repainting, reroofing, laying new carpet, landscaping, plumbing, and so on.

In the end, you have a property that is very much improved and worth more money. Your partner has saved a lot of his valuable time. He didn't have to spend all his free time renovating the property. You saved $5,000 and got some exercise. You both have gained because after the renovation, the property obviously has much greater value.

Sweat equity can be used in many different investment areas. Instead of working on a property, you may be able to make an agreement in which you manage the property for a designated time. Or if you and a partner are thinking of going into business, you can work out a deal where he comes up with the initial investment and you work in the business, in lieu of putting your share of the cash up front.

It is a good idea to make a detailed list beforehand of the work you will be required to do, or the amount of hours you will have to work to fulfill your half of the bargain. If all this is spelled out ahead of time, you may save a lot of bickering later on.

How Much You Can Raise

The only limits are your skills and your available time. Raising more than $20,000 or $30,000 might be difficult— you would have to work and sweat a long time to repay that much money.

How Fast

The other person's money is paid up front. You pay it back through your labor at whatever rate you have agreed upon.

Credit Needed

One of the major benefits of sweat equity is that anyone can do it, regardless of their credit rating, since no actual borrowing is involved. Your partner, or the person you are buying the property or business from, has to have enough confidence in you to front the money initially.

Advantages

This is one of the best ways for young people to get involved in businesses or rental properties without having to come up with a lot of cash. While you're young, you have a lot of time, energy, and enthusiasm. You can use these qualities to build up a rental property investment, without needing a lot of cash. You may also learn some valuable skills along the way!

DISADVANTAGES

The main problem with a sweat equity agreement is that you are locked into a certain amount of labor. Your circumstances may unexpectedly change, and it could become difficult for you to get the work done as agreed upon. Also, you may not have many of the skills necessary to renovate a piece of property. Not everyone can do plumbing or carpet laying. If you choose this plan, make sure that the agreement is written out carefully beforehand and is not just some sort of verbal understanding. You don't want to get into arguments later about how much time you will spend working and what you have to accomplish. The better the agreement is spelled out now, the less open it is to interpretation and disagreement later. In fact, you should consider asking an attorney to help you draw up an agreement; you would have to pay a legal fee, but it could save you from costly misunderstandings.

#34. Have Loan Payments to You Accelerated at a Discount

Does anyone owe you any money? Maybe you can get that money back, *fast!* Let's say that you loaned $3,000 to a friend for some purpose, and he agreed to pay you back over two years. Or you sold him a car, a boat, or a piece of land and agreed to receive your money in monthly payments. Now, you need the money fast for some emergency, and he has the ability to pay you back in full.

You can approach him like this: Offer to let him repay the loan, right now, in full, for only $2,700. That is, you give him a 10 percent discount as an incentive to pay in full immediately. Use whatever discount you choose: you can offer 2 percent, 5 percent, 10 percent, 20 percent, whatever. If he is a very good friend and can see your plight, he may offer to pay the loan back right away with no incentive at all. Either way, you get the idea of loan repayment at a discount.

How Much You Can Raise
This depends on how much you have previously loaned out to others.

How Fast
Just as fast as your debtors can get the money from their bank to pay you back. They may even want to take out a loan to pay you back because of the discount incentive.

Credit Needed
Your credit rating doesn't matter.

Advantages
You can get the money pretty fast without dealing with any lending-institution red tape.

Disadvantages
There are several disadvantages to this money-raising plan. First of all, it assumes that you have loaned out money to someone in the first place. Next, you get back only 85 to 95 percent of your invested dollar—not a good way to get rich! Finally, you depend upon someone else to repay you immediately, which may not be possible at this time. There are much better ways to raise cash than to have your loans prepaid at a discount, but this is an alternative if you have exhausted the more conventional ways.

#35. Garage Sale or Swapmeet

How about raising money fast and cleaning out your garage at the same time? If you need to raise anywhere from $100 to $1,000 in the next week, try a garage sale or swapmeet.

First, go through your entire home and collect the things that you no longer want or use, or that no longer fit you. Go through all the closets, cupboards, your garage, and your other storage areas. The more items you can find, the more money you will make. A good rule of thumb when cleaning out your closets is: If you haven't worn it in a year, get rid of it!

Now, put an ad in the local newspaper and put up signs in your area advertising your garage or yard sale. The best time to hold a garage sale is on a weekend. Start Saturday morning at about seven o'clock, and remain open until about four in the afternoon, when the business finally begins to die down. Follow approximately the same hours on Sunday. Most of your profits will be made on Saturday, since that is the day when most garage sale followers will visit.

A swapmeet works much the same way. Pack all your items into a car or truck and drive to the local swapmeet, which is usually held in a drive-in theater or other large parking lot. At a swapmeet, you are side by side with hundreds of other sellers. Even with the competition, you could still make a lot of money. Remember, your "junk" is unique.

How Much You Can Raise

This depends entirely on how much you have to sell and the success of the sale. When I have participated in garage sales in the past, I have made between $200 and $500 over a single weekend.

How Fast

You can raise the money by next weekend.

Credit Needed

Your credit rating doesn't matter.

Advantages

The advantages are many. First, you can unclutter your house or garage (which is always a good idea) and raise cash at the same time. Second, the time frame is quick. You can hold a garage sale next weekend if you choose. Third, you can collect fast cash without going into debt.

Disadvantages

The disadvantages are mainly the inconvenience of holding a sale in your yard. You may not want people trampling all over your lawn. Moreover, a garage sale usually blows your whole weekend.

#36. Government Grant

A grant is simply a gift of money for a specific purpose that is deemed worthy. It differs from a loan in that you never have to pay it back. It is simply a free gift.

The U.S. government gives out billions of dollars in grants every year, for myriad purposes that the government wants to promote. The National Endowment for the Arts, for example, has an annual budget of about $170 million, most of which is given out in grants to various artists around the country. There are also education grants (see number 27), minority grants, housing grants, business grants, and other general welfare grants.

An excellent article on these grants and how to apply for them was written by Steve Rogers in the September 1989 issue of *Wealth* magazine (2801 Camino del Rio South, San Diego CA 92108, 619-297-8500). You can get further information on government grants from your local library, although it takes some digging.

To apply for a grant, fill out your application and proposal letter as professionally as possible and send it in. You may want to apply to many different grant programs, as you will be in competition with dozens, perhaps even hundreds of other people. Your odds of getting a grant increase with the number of them you apply for.

How Much You Can Raise

Most grants are in the $1,000-to-$20,000 range. Some grants can be for hundreds of thousands of dollars for certain types, such as small business grants.

How Fast

Getting a grant takes some time. After you have sent in your application, you may not hear the outcome for several months. This plan may not be the best if you need the money right away.

Credit Needed

Your credit should not be a factor since the money doesn't have to be repaid.

Advantages

The main advantage is that a grant is free money that never has to be repaid. The U.S. government simply provides this money to projects and purposes that it deems worthy and important. You don't need to have good credit or other assets because there is no loan involved—so just about any U.S. citizen may apply.

Disadvantages

Since there is so much competition, your odds of getting a government grant are not the best. You can increase your odds by applying for several different grants at the same time. Why not, as long as they are giving away free money? Another disadvantage of grants is the time frame involved. If you need the money right away, you may not be able to wait several months for it.

#37. Take on a Partner

You have found a piece of real estate or a business opportunity that's just too good to pass up, but you don't have the cash available to swing the deal. What can you do?

One answer may be to take on a partner. Find a person who is willing to bankroll part (or all) of the costs in exchange for part of the profits. The great thing about partners is that they don't always have to be fifty-fifty. You may find someone who will supply all the capital for a project in return for only one-half or one-third of the return. Your contribution to the investment may be your business or management skills alone. Many investors are willing to finance young, eager entrepreneurs. They have the capital, while you have the time, drive, and energy to make the business or property a financial success.

Think for a moment of everyone you know who might be willing to put up money to be a partner in a business or real estate venture. I believe that anyone can think of a few prospective wealthy partners. Put your mind to it. When you have a list of possible partners, put together a business plan. How much do you need to make the enterprise succeed? What will be your part of the partnership? How will you earn your share? For how long will you need the money? How can the partner get his money out of the business, if necessary? What kind of return do you expect? In short, put down on paper the answers to all the questions a potential partner will have. The more professional your business plan looks, the more likely you are to lure investors to your idea.

How Much You Can Raise

The sky is the limit! A good business or real estate plan will draw investors to you. Remember to do your homework and write up a lengthy business proposal. The more complete and professional your plan appears, the more money you may be able to raise.

How Fast

If potential partners like your ideas and plans, they may want to invest immediately. The money may become available as fast as you can tell investors about your plan.

Credit Needed

Obviously, if you have great credit, use this to your advantage. Show potential partners your credit history: how you've always been responsible in paying your debts. If your credit is poor, don't bring it up. (But, of course, if you are asked about it, you must answer honestly.)

Advantages

There are several advantages to having partners. First of all, you may be able to secure a large piece of the action with very little of your own money. Second, if you are dealing with people you know, there will be very little formality and red tape. (Still, it is a good idea to have a lawyer draw up the partnership documents, as he may raise questions that you never thought of.) Third, because of this informality, you may be able to get the money very quickly.

DISADVANTAGES

With partners, you put up less of your own money, but you also surrender a piece of the potential profits. You may not want to give away a portion of your business or property. Another thing to think about is that you give away a portion of the authority to your partners. You don't have the final say so on every subject. You may dislike having to discuss major matters with all the partners. You may come to resent it, and that could take a lot of the fun out of running your own business or property. Think honestly about whether or not you are the kind of individual who could come to dislike a partnership because you want to run the show alone.

#38. Venture Capitalist

If you are trying to raise cash in order to create a new product or business idea, you may want to consider using a venture capital company. Venture capitalists are wealthy individuals or groups that invest in new businesses and products. Major companies such as Apple Computer were begun with the backing of venture capital firms.

In order to secure the financial backing of a venture capitalist, you must first do your homework. If you have devised a new product or process, make up a prototype and invest the money necessary to get a patent. Protect your idea, if you believe in it.

Then write up a business plan. Spend some time thinking about the possible markets for your product or business. Work out some numbers. Maybe even have an accountant or lawyer help you create a professional business package. Venture capitalists see many, many new ideas, and they are not impressed easily. Don't approach one with a half-baked plan. Do the homework necessary to prepare a professional business proposal.

You can find the names and addresses of many venture capital firms in the classified sections of magazines such as *Venture, Entrepreneur, Success, Inc., Income Opportunities* magazine, and the like. Your local library may have lists of venture capital companies—ask for assistance in finding them. You can also look in the business sections of major metropolitan newspapers and in *The Wall Street Journal*. You may even find them in your local phone book.

Once you have found a venture capital firm that is willing to back you up with financing, make an appointment with a lawyer to set up all the details—preferably an attorney who has handled this kind of agreement before.

Venture capitalists aren't frivolous with their money. They back only new products or businesses that have a very good chance of succeeding, and they don't come cheap. In repayment for their initial backing, they generally become fifty-fifty partners in your company. Venture money firms try to get a return of at least 100 percent and as much as 500 percent for the money they invest. They can earn such large returns because they take the risk to invest in fledgling businesses and products that no conventional banker would touch.

How Much You Can Raise

If your product or idea merits it, you can raise millions of dollars through venture capitalists. The key is to come up with a tremendous new idea and then find a venture company that will back you up.

How Fast

The time that passes from when you come up with the original idea to when you actually have money in your hands may be as little as a couple months to as much as a year or two. This is not the place to go if you need money overnight.

CREDIT NEEDED
Your previous credit is not the main criterion with venture capitalists. Your product or invention and your business plan are.

ADVANTAGES
Along with backing you financially, venture capital firms will do everything in their power to help your business grow. After all, the more you prosper, the more money they make, too, since they own a piece of the business. Also, venture firms will loan you vast amounts of money if your idea warrants it—much more than you likely could ever raise in any other way.

DISADVANTAGES
Venture capitalists aren't in the business of charity. They rightly expect to be very well paid for the risks they take. If you do not want to surrender a portion of your business or product in order to raise cash, look for funds from some other area. Another problem is that it may take quite a long time before you get your funding through a venture capital firm. If your idea is a timely one, you may not have the time to wait.

#39. Form a Syndicate

If you are trying to raise large amounts of money to buy rental property, a business, or some other substantial investment, you may want to form a syndicate. You hear about large real estate syndicates all the time. These are simply groups of investors who put up different amounts of money to buy pieces of the total investment.

Let's say, for example, that you want to buy an apartment building for $100,000. You could sell one hundred shares in the property to other investors for $1,000 apiece. Each individual investor can buy as many shares as he chooses, although you may want to hold a certain number of shares aside for yourself so you can maintain control over the investment. As a matter of fact, you may want to sell 105 or 110 shares of the syndicate—the extra $5,000 or $10,000 going to you for setting up the whole deal (a good business idea!). This can become a great way to invest in real estate or business without putting up any of your own money.

Use a good lawyer to set up the plan. For example, the agreement should contain provisions for cashing out individual investors if they need the money, selling the investment, the target price, where the business or rental profits will go in the meantime, and so on. Think through the entire investment, and make plans ahead of time for every eventuality.

Syndicates are a great way to raise large amounts of money. Billions of dollars are invested in them in the United States today!

How Much You Can Raise

You can raise literally millions of dollars, if your syndicate attracts enough investors. Raising smaller amounts, such as $50,000 to $250,000, should be relatively easy through word of mouth alone.

How Fast

It may take several months to raise the cash you need through a syndicate.

Credit Needed

Your personal credit may not be a factor in forming a syndicate. But if you've ever failed to pay someone back, you may have trouble interesting potential investors in your plan.

Advantages

Forming a syndicate may allow you to raise incredible amounts of cash in a very short time. You may even be able to pay yourself for creating and managing the syndicate. Your syndicate can simply be a group of friends and relatives, or you may want to advertise for potential investors from all over the country.

Disadvantages

By obtaining money from others through a syndicate, you

are surrendering part of your management control of the investment. In other words, if you have twenty investors in your syndicate, you will have twenty different opinions as to how to manage that investment. You may not want that many differing opinions to think about. Also, some investors may need to get out before the end of the investment, and you will have to have funds to cash them out. By setting up a good, solid business plan through a lawyer, you can foresee many problems and agree ahead of time on procedures to work them out.

#40. Sell your Equity

If you own something of value—like a car, a house, a boat, a piece of rental property, or a business—you may be able to sell part of your equity to raise fast cash. This is like taking on a partner, but it's also different in that you are just raising money and using whatever you have of value as the collateral. The person who loans you the money buys the equity—he doesn't take the item of value.

For example, you decide to sell part of the interest you have in an automobile. You get a loan from a friend or relative and give the certificate of title to them. You keep the car—they have the title and the legal right to take and sell the car if you don't pay them back. Or you sell someone one-half the value of your car and make arrangements for both of you to use it. That way, you still keep the car, and you get some cash.

With a house or rental property it basically works the

same way. If you have $10,000 equity in the property, you could sell one-half of your share to someone for $5,000. Just go to a lawyer or escrow company, and have them draw up the documents. The charge for this should be very small—$25 to $50. As soon as the papers are signed, you have $5,000 in your hand, tax free, and you still own one-half of the property. You can even sell part of your real estate equity in exchange for the tax benefits. For example, you may be able to find a wealthy investor who is concerned only with getting the rental property tax write-off. He may not be interested in the cash flow at all! Make sure you don't sell part of your real estate too cheaply, as this type of investment will most likely continue to go up in value.

If someone purchases one-half of your equity in a business, he is usually entitled to one-half of the cash flow (profits) and one-half of the selling price when the business is sold. Again, don't sell equity in a business too cheaply. There may be better ways to raise cash than to give up a portion of something for which you have worked for a long time.

How Much You Can Raise

This depends on how much equity you have in an item, and how much equity you can sell to someone (a half, a third, a tenth, or what have you). You can probably raise anywhere from $1,000 to hundreds of thousands of dollars.

How Fast

You can do it as fast as you can find someone with available cash who is willing to purchase your equity. It may be a friend or relative, or you may want to find someone by placing an ad in the paper advertising the type of equity you want to sell.

CREDIT NEEDED

Since no actual borrowing is involved, your credit history should not be an issue.

ADVANTAGES

The advantages are many. First, you are not actually borrowing the money, so you can make any arrangements regarding paying it back. Or you may choose not to pay it back at all, and just let the other party keep the equity in the item that you sold. You are not dealing with a bank or other financial institution, so the red tape is kept at a minimum. Finally, you may be able to raise a very substantial amount of money (especially if you are selling the equity in a piece of real estate or a business).

DISADVANTAGES

When you sell part of your equity, you are also selling two other things—complete control over the object or investment, and future gains you may have realized. For example, if you sell part of your rental property equity, you raise cash but you lose absolute control over the property. You have another person to deal with when making decisions. You also have to split the profits in the property when it comes time to sell (unless you have worked out other arrangements). This could cost you a lot of potential profit, so it may be better to raise money in another way.

#41. Get a Co-Signer

If for some reason you cannot qualify for a loan on your own (because you have no previous credit, you're too young, or you have a bad credit history), you may want to try to qualify by getting a co-signer. A co-signer is a person who signs along with you on a loan and in effect shoulders the repayment responsibility with you.

Financial institutions may ask you for a co-signer as a last resort if they are trying to make you a loan but you just don't qualify according to their lending criteria. They generally like a co-signer to be your close relative, such as a mother or father, or sister or brother. Lenders know that family members will stand by someone a lot longer than friends usually will.

If you have previously had really terrible credit, in most cases, getting a co-signer will not help you. A co-signer is more often used in the case of a young person trying to get a loan for the first time, or in the case of someone with very limited credit history or financial instability.

How Much You Can Raise

Generally when you are using a co-signer, the amount you can borrow will be limited since the lender may have to rely on your co-signer to repay the loan if you can't or won't.

How Fast

A co-signed loan may take an extra day or two because of the extra credit checking and paperwork required.

Credit Needed

Usually you need a co-signer because of poor or no previous credit.

Advantages

Using a co-signer, such as a parent, to help get a loan for the first time is a good way for young people to start out. It gives them the opportunity to establish credit when no lender would normally loan them money on their own.

Disadvantages

There are several disadvantages. First, if you cannot or will not make the payments for some reason, your co-signer will be required to. If you are late making your payments, this will reflect on your co-signer's credit record as well as yours. This may place an unfair burden on your co-signer. If payment problems begin, co-signing may cause rifts between friends or family members. Think over the responsibility you are placing on a friend or relative before you ask them to co-sign a loan for you. By all means, do everything in your power to pay back the loan in full and on time. This will look good on your credit record as well as your co-signer's.

#42. Finance Company

If you have gone to a bank for a loan and been turned down, your next stop could be a finance company. Finance companies go by different names in different states, such as thrifts, thrift and loans, and names that end in the word *finance* or *financial* (as in AVCO Finance). These institutions generally specialize in making loans that are substandard by normal banking criteria, loans that the traditional banking community passes up because the loans are too small, the borrowers' previous credit is poor, the length of the loan is too long or too short, and so on. Since finance companies make these substandard loans, financial regulators allow them to charge much higher interest rates than regular banks can charge. Banks are normally limited (again, it depends upon which state you live in) to 21 percent maximum interest on their loans. Finance companies can charge up to 25 or 35 percent.

Since finance companies make loans that other lenders

will not touch, they usually require collateral of some type. The collateral can be the title to your car (regardless of its age), or a lien against your furniture, appliances, television, stereo system, and so on.

To give you an idea of what you would have to pay: On a one-year $1,500 loan at 28 percent, your payments would be $160 per month, and the total interest would come to $420. There are a lot cheaper ways to raise money!

How Much You Can Raise

Usually you can raise only $5,000 to $10,000. Most finance company loans are in the $1,000-to-$3,000 range.

How Fast

You can usually get such a loan within about five working days.

Credit Needed

Some previous credit will usually be necessary, even if it was poor.

Advantages

The main advantage to using a finance company is that it may make you a loan when no one else will.

Disadvantages

You will pay a very high interest rate for the privilege of borrowing—between 20 and 35 percent. The loan-payback periods may be short, which will make the payments relatively high compared with the amount borrowed. You may have to pledge some type of collateral, so if you get behind in your payments, the finance company can repossess the item and sell it to pay off the loan. Using a finance company can even *hurt* your credit in the short run. Some bankers actually look down on finance company loans and count them against you in the future.

#43. Credit Union

If you ever have the opportunity to join a credit union, by all means do so. A credit union is an organization of savers who are all affiliated in some way, such as through their job, church, or other institution. Since credit unions are generally nonprofit organizations, the interest rate you pay on loans is lower than at conventional banks, and the interest paid to you on your savings is higher.

Another reason to become associated with a credit union is that its lending practices may be a bit more lenient, since it knows you better and may place greater faith in your repayment ability. Join your credit union if the opportunity exists. If nothing else, you are opening up an alternative lending institution.

ADVANTAGES

Here are several reasons to join your local credit union:

- a possible source for loans (It never hurts to have many lenders available to you when you need them.);
- possibly lower loan rates;
- possibly a better chance of qualifying for loans since you are dealing with people you know (rather than people at a large bank where you are just a number);
- the possibility that the credit union may be able to take your loan payments directly out of your paycheck every month, saving you the hassle of sending in the payment monthly and preventing late payments;
- higher interest paid on your savings.

DISADVANTAGES

Banking with people you know well can be a two-edged sword. One disadvantage is that your private financial situation (and possible problems) may be looked into by fellow workers and other people you know. You may not want to surrender your financial privacy, regardless of the benefits. Another disadvantage is that most credit union loans contain a provision called the "right of offset." This means that if you are late on your payments to the credit union, it can take the money directly out of your checking or savings account. This could create some real problems for you if you go through a period of financial difficulty and get a little behind on your payments.

#44. Start a Small Part-Time Business

An excellent way to bring in a lot of extra cash is to begin a small business of your own. There are hundreds of small, easy-to-start businesses that don't take a lot of money to begin, but they can bring in a substantial part-time income.

Think of all the things you are good at or have done in the past for a living. What would you enjoy trying on a part-time basis? Sit down and make a list of all your abilities. What do you know how to do that could be made into an income-producing part-time job?

Here is just a sample list of the many business that you can begin on a shoestring to start earning some big part-time income right away:

- Got a chainsaw and some clippers? How about a tree-trimming business?

- Got a truck or a trailer? How about a hauling business?
- Got a squeegee and some sponges and buckets? How about beginning a window-washing service?
- Love to clean cars? Why not begin an automobile-detailing service?
- Got a lawn mower and edger? How about a lawn-care business?
- Know how to fly planes or sail a boat? Why not become an instructor?
- Great at mathematics or a foreign language? You can tutor students who are having a hard time in these subjects!
- Love to make crafts? Why not sell them at local shops and fairs?
- Got a video camera? Why not start a wedding video service?
- Like to work outside in the sunshine? Why not begin a pool-cleaning business?
- Do you have your own tools, and are you a good mechanic? Why not start a mobile tune-up service?
- Got a pickup or van? How about a cross-town moving or delivery service?

These twelve businesses can be started for just a few dollars, and each has the potential to make a very large part-time income for you. Many of these businesses can be started with trucks, tools, or other equipment that you may already have—cutting your startup costs even more.

To get hundreds of other small business ideas, get a copy of *Entrepreneur* magazine. Each issue is packed full of small business ideas. Your local library or bookstore has dozens of books on starting and running a small business.

You have nothing to lose by starting up a small part-time business. You can begin in many cases with less than a hundred dollars and be out making extra money by your next day off.

How Much You Can Raise

Many people begin a part-time business to earn some extra money and find themselves earning more than they do in their full-time careers. The only thing that limits your income is how much time you can devote to your part-time business.

How Fast

You can begin earning extra money on your next day off.

Credit Needed

Your credit rating doesn't matter.

Advantages

There are many. First, you can get extra money without borrowing. Second, you are building up a small business that not only pays you income now, but is valuable in itself. Once you build up a business, complete with all the necessary equipment and a regular customer base, it can be sold to a new owner for a percentage of the annual income it produces. Next, many tax deductions are available to self-employed people, even if their small enterprise does not show a large profit. Check with your accountant or tax preparer for more complete information regarding home-based business tax deductions. Finally, you may build up a part-time business that is so lucrative, it can replace your regular job, and you can begin working for yourself on a full-time basis. Many people dream of being their own boss. If you have ever felt that way, give it a try. You may end up wondering why you waited so long.

DISADVANTAGES

You may not have the skills or the temperament to go out on your own in a part-time business. Also, you may not want to spend your free time working on another job. You may need your free time for other activities.

#45. Cancel or Cash in Items

Do you have a deposit on file for a car, boat, vacation, or club membership, that can be canceled to get some money back? Think about it for a while. You may have paid deposits to utility companies to get services installed or turned on. The deposit is just to insure that you pay your bill in a timely manner. If you have paid right on time for several months or years, you can call the utility and ask to have your deposit returned. There may be dozens of items for which you have deposits on file, and they may add up to hundreds or even thousands of dollars. For example:

- water company
- gas company
- electric company
- telephone company
- trash removal service
- cable TV company

- bottled water service
- security deposit to your landlord (if you are a renter)

As you can see, you use many services that may be holding a substantial deposit from you. Call them and ask if they can be returned. They may turn you down, but if you have paid your bills on time in the past, the companies may feel secure enough to return your money.

Next; Is there anything you can cancel to get money back? Take some time to think about this one. For example, if you really need to cut expenses and raise cash, how about canceling these items:

- health or country club membership
- magazine or newsletter subscriptions
- book clubs
- co-ops (such as membership stores)
- orders for a new car, equipment, household goods, computer, or boat
- merchandise that you have bought and aren't happy with.

I realize that this is quite a varied list, but I'm trying to give you a wide range of ideas of items that you can cancel in order to get some money back. Take a little time to think about all the things in your life that you can cancel or return in order to cut expenses and raise cash.

How Much You Can Raise

This obviously depends on how much deposit money you have paid out in the past. Most Americans have at least several hundred dollars in deposit money on file with various companies.

How Fast

You can raise this usually within a couple of weeks. But keep in mind that you are dealing with bureaucracies, and they can move very slowly. After all, you are asking a favor of them.

Credit Needed

You have to have paid your bills in a timely manner in order for the companies involved to return your deposits.

Advantages

Since money on deposit usually does not earn interest, it is better to have that money in your savings account than in the bank account of the utility company. If you pay all your bills on time, the utility company doesn't need a deposit. Also, it's always better to use your own money in raising cash.

Disadvantages

The only disadvantage to this plan is that you are losing the cushion you have in case you ever have a problem making your utility or rental payments. With no deposit money on file, companies are less eager to give you extra time to make your payments.

#46. Borrow to Buy Gold, Silver, and Rare Coins

If you are trying to raise money in order to invest in precious metals, you can borrow the money directly and quite easily. Several banks now offer plans that loan you 75 to 80 percent of the value of the gold, silver, platinum, or rare numismatic coins that you want to buy.

Your local coin or precious metals dealer will probably know of one or two financial institutions that have gold and silver loan plans. It is relatively easy to get this type of loan since the bank will hold the precious metals as collateral until you repay the loan. The bank's risk is virtually nil (other than the possibility that the actual value of the bullion will drop below the loan amount—and even that would require a 20 to 25 percent drop in the price of the metals as the bank only lends 75 to 80 percent of the original value).

How Much You Can Raise

Anywhere from $1,000 to tens of thousands of dollars can be raised.

How Fast

This type of loan can usually be approved within a couple of business days, unless the amount you are trying to borrow is quite substantial.

Credit Needed

You can get this type of loan even if your credit is terrible, since the bank is loaning only about 75 to 80 percent of the bullion value.

Advantages

This loan program allows you to purchase and invest in gold, silver, and rare coins with only 20 to 25 percent of your own money. Such use of leverage can greatly increase your profits. For example, if you buy gold bullion with 20 percent down and the price of gold then goes up 20 percent, you make a 100 percent profit on the money you have invested! Although you are speculating somewhat by purchasing the bullion with only a fraction of the money necessary to buy, you still have the choice to sell or to continue to hold. This differs from futures and options contracts, where you are speculating and can be forced to liquidate your position if the price of the metal drops below a certain price.

Disadvantages

First, many investors buy gold and silver as a calamity hedge. If there is major war, a natural disaster, uncontrolled inflation, or a social upheaval, precious metals become an excellent type of insurance. The problem is that you want to have the metals in your home safe or other secret place—not sitting in a bank vault, where you may not be able to reach them in time of emergency. Having the bank hold the bullion as collateral entirely defeats the purpose of many investors. Also, for as long as the loan is in effect, you will be paying interest, making your bullion purchase more expensive.

#47. Use a Mortgage Broker

If you are trying to purchase a piece of real estate, and you are having some trouble getting a loan, you may want to use a mortgage broker. A mortgage broker is simply a person who earns a commission by setting up mortgage loans. He may work with several lenders and may therefore have a better shot at getting a loan for you. His fee is taken out of the closing costs you pay when you buy a property. Since he has to add his commission to the normal bank fees, your costs may be higher when using a mortgage broker.

You can find mortgage brokers through referrals either from your real estate salesman or from a broker, through ads in the paper, or through the phone book. A mortgage broker will usually come to your home or business to help you set up the loan, so you don't have to run all over town. After he takes the necessary information, he puts a loan package together and sends it to his loan committee. Since his only source of income is setting up loans for consumers, he will do everything in his power to get your loan approved.

How Much You Can Raise

Most lenders will loan up to 80 or 90 percent of the purchase price of most types of real estate.

How Fast

Mortgage lenders are notorious for taking a long time. Figure on at least four to six weeks before the loan is funded. If you need quick cash, this may not be the best way to go.

Credit Needed

You usually need reasonably good credit to qualify for a home loan. There are many programs, however, for potential home buyers with poor previous credit.

Advantages

First, using a mortgage broker is convenient. He or she will normally come to you—you don't have to go to them. Next, by using a mortgage broker, you have one more person on your side pushing for you. After all, he won't get paid unless the loan is funded. He may be able to package and structure a loan so it will be more readily accepted by lenders. He may even be able to speed up the loan a bit by doing a lot of the legwork himself, rather than mailing out documents.

Disadvantages

Using a mortgage broker may cost you several thousand dollars extra. He will normally charge one to one-and-a-half points (a point is 1 percent of the loan amount). Therefore, if your broker charges 1 point on a $120,000 loan, his fee (and your added cost) will be $1,200! This may be worth it if you cannot get a mortgage loan any other way. Another disadvantage is that, unfortunately, many mortgage brokers promise more than they can deliver. They may not be able to set up a loan for you, but leave you hanging in the meantime, wondering if you will get the loan or not.

CAUTION

Don't ever use a mortgage broker who needs a fee "up front" just to get the paperwork going. This is a tip-off that he will not do much of anything about getting you a home loan, and at worst, he may be running a scam. If your broker needs money up front, drop him and find someone else. Think about it for a moment. If a mortgage broker charges each customer a $200 upfront fee and talks to fifteen or twenty potential borrowers every month, he will make $3,000 to $4,000 in a single month. With such an income, why would he ever need to actually set up a loan for anyone? He would make a good living on the upfront fees alone!

#48. Pawnshop

A very quick way to raise cash is to use a pawnshop. You can take most anything of value (coins, firearms, jewelry, tools, musical instruments, typewriters, and the like) to a pawnbroker and walk away with cash.

A pawnshop loans you money against property that you put up for collateral (usually 25 to 50 percent of the value of an item). Say, for example, that you decide to pawn some tools that have a value of $800. A pawnbroker will probably loan you $200 to $400 at most. You can "redeem" you property anytime in the next six months by paying back the loan plus interest, usually 30 to 60 percent annually. So your loan of $200 will end up costing you between $30 to $60 in interest charges over the six-month period. If you don't reclaim and pay off your property within the designated period, the pawnbroker has the right to offer your property for sale.

How Much You Can Raise

You can raise anywhere from $25 to $2,500 or even more. It depends on the value of the property you put up as collateral.

How Fast

You get paid immediately, in cash!

Credit Needed

Your credit is no problem when using pawnbrokers. That's part of their attractiveness.

Advantages

Speed and ease are the main advantages to using a pawnshop. You get your money in a matter of minutes. You can pawn practically anything of value, and you don't have to qualify for a loan to get money. You are simply pledging your own property (at a three-to-one or four-to-one ratio) against the loan. This may be a good way to raise cash if you have property against which you want to borrow but that you don't want to sell. Another advantage to using pawnbrokers is that you can borrow relatively small amounts of money (even as low as $10!) and can repay the loan in a week or as late as six months.

Disadvantages

One disadvantage is that you can borrow only about one-fourth or one-third of the value of your property, so you have to pawn an awful lot of stuff to raise much money. Second, if you can't pay the money back for some reason, your property will be sold to someone else. Third, pawnshops charge astronomical interest rates.

#49. Reverse Annuity Mortgage

If you own your home outright and you need cash, but you don't want to sell your home or take out a loan, you may want to look into the reverse annuity mortgage, or RAM. The RAM works just the opposite of a conventional mortgage loan. With a conventional loan, you make a large down payment, then make monthly payments until the property is paid off. With a RAM, the bank pays you a lump sum now, then makes monthly payments to you until you either sell the home or die (in which case, the bank is repaid from the proceeds of your estate). Instead of building up equity every month, as with a normal mortgage, you are slowly eating up your equity now instead of leaving it to your heirs.

This arrangement may seem unusual, but it works very well for people who are retired and "house rich" but can't afford to take out a loan and make monthly payments, and don't want to sell out and move.

Here's how a RAM works: Let's assume you have a free and clear home worth $100,000. You can probably arrange a RAM that pays you $5,000 to $20,000 up front now, and several hundred dollars per month until you either sell the home or die. This monthly income can be used to supplement your usual retirement or pension income.

For further information on reverse annuity mortgages, you can write to the American Association of Retired Persons (AARP), Home Equity Information Center, 1909 K Street N.W., Washington DC 20049, or to HUD, Single Family Development Division, Room 9272, 451 7th Street S.W., Washington DC 20410.

How Much You Can Raise

You can probably get several thousand dollars immediately, then a steady flow of income for the rest of your life to help supplement your Social Security and any other retirement or pension income you have.

How Fast

You can usually have the entire transaction wrapped up within four to six weeks.

Credit Needed

Your credit rating is of little consequence since the bank is making payments to you, not the reverse. The bank is mainly interested in the equity in your home.

Advantages

There are many. Millions of senior citizens live in homes that are paid off or nearly paid off, yet they don't qualify or can't afford a conventional loan. They are "house rich" but can't afford to tap into their equity with a conventional loan and make payments. A RAM is the answer. Not only do you get a lump sum now, you get monthly payments for the rest of your life.

Disadvantages

Obviously, not everyone has a lot of equity in their home,

so they wouldn't qualify for a RAM. Second, many seniors consider their paid-off home to be their major asset, and they dislike the idea of living off the equity in it. They would actually be living off equity that would be passed on to their heirs eventually. To many retired people, leaving money to their children or grandchildren is very important, so they don't want to use that money now on themselves. Finally, be sure to check with your accountant or another professional about the tax consequences of the RAM.

#50. Loan Broker

If you are trying to raise cash in order to start a new business, develop a product, or even buy some real estate, you may want to try using a loan broker. Loan brokers are intermediaries between organizations that want to loan money to worthy projects, and individuals or small companies who need money. You can find a loan broker either through your telephone book, under "Loans" (look for listings that appear to be from private individuals, not financial institutions), or through the classified section of a major metropoliatan newspaper or *The Wall Street Journal*, under listings such as "Money to Lend."

Loan brokers can help arrange loans that conventional lenders have turned down. They are paid a small portion of the proceeds as their commission. On a $20,000 loan, for example, their fee may be 10 percent of the loan amount. This may seem a bit excessive, but keep in mind that loan brokers help get loans for people who have been turned down by most other lenders. Their fee percentage usually declines as the loan amount increases. Some loan brokers also charge a small nonrefundable fee of perhaps $100 to handle your loan and to take care of all the paperwork.

How Much You Can Raise

Loan brokers specialize in large loans—anywhere from $10,000 to $200,000 or even more. Their commission starts at 8 to 10 percent for smaller loans and usually drops to about 2 percent on larger loans.

How Fast

Obtaining the money may take several weeks or months, as the broker will try to get the loan through several different sources.

Credit Needed

Obtaining money through a loan broker is unusual. Loan brokers do not deal with conventional lenders, so your past credit history may not be as important. As a matter of fact, many businessmen who use loan brokers to obtain funds have ruined their credit in a past business failure and are forced to go this route.

Advantages

A loan broker may be able to get several hundred thousand dollars for you, if your business idea or investment makes sense. The broker is paid only if he gets you the money, so you don't lose a thing by trying. Also, to earn his fee, he takes care of all the document preparation and does all the legwork. You can let him do all the running around. Further, your loan broker can send your loan paperwork to dozens of potential lenders that you don't even know about. He may have literally hundreds of sources for loans.

Disadvantages

The main disadvantage to using a loan broker is that a

large fee comes out of your proceeds for the broker. For example, on a $50,000 loan, his fee could be between 8 and 10 percent, so your cost could be $4,000 to $5,000! This may still be worthwhile because a loan broker may be able to get you thousands of dollars more than you could get through any other source.

#51. Keep the Rebate!

If you are in the market for a new car, there's a way to buy a car and get money back! Here's how it works.

For the last ten years or so, most major automobile manufacturers have offered rebates to induce customers to buy new cars. At times, these rebates have been pretty substantial—ranging from $2,500 up to $5,000! The rebates vary on different models, and the more expensive makes have the higher rebates, but even lower-priced family-type vehicles have had rebates in the $1,500 to $3,000 range.

Judging from my own experience as a finance manager for a car dealer, most people use these rebates as part of their down payment on the car in order to lower their monthly payments. A dealer may even try to coerce you into doing this. The good news is that you don't have to! You really can "buy a car, get a check," as Lee Iacocca used to say in the Chrysler commercials.

Here's how to do it. First of all, when a bank finances your new car, it will normally finance the invoice amount of the car (the amount that the dealer paid to the factory), plus tax and license. The car salesman will probably press you to put down a large down payment because the larger the down payment you make, the larger the potential profit to the dealer. You see, since the lender usually finances only the dealer's cost of an automobile, the dealer's profit comes from the down payment. Small down payments mean small profits. Large down payments mean large potential profits to the dealer.

The lender wants you to make a large down payment too, because it gives you a vested interest in making your future payments. For example, a person who puts down $5,000 when he buys a new car is a lot more likely to make his car payments, even if it requires a sacrifice, than the person who puts down only $500. People who put down a very small down payment have less to lose if they stop making payments and the car is repossessed.

That is the bank's point of view. But if you're a reliable person with a decent credit standing, there is no reason for you to make a massive down payment. It's better for you to keep your extra money in the bank for emergencies and have a slightly higher car payment, than it is to make a giant down payment to make the bank and the car dealer happy.

That's where the rebate fits in. The dealer will try to use it as a sales incentive, as though he were the one giving it to you. The dealer may say something like, "The price of the car comes to $13,450 including the tax and license. Then after subtracting the $2,000 factory rebate, your cost comes down to only $11,450 out the door. Do we have a deal?" The dealer has used the rebate as a negotiating tool. Instead of giving you a discount, he simply subtracted the factory rebate to make the deal better. But keep in mind that you get the rebate no matter what kind of deal you work out with the dealer. Don't even let the rebate come into the negotiation. Think of it as a nice little bonus for having been a knowledgeable shopper.

Rebates come and go with amazing regularity. The minute they are discontinued, new car sales fall. Then sales managers at the Big Three automakers (GM, Ford, and Chrysler) begin to panic, and a new round of rebates is announced—always "for a limited time only." Since rebates have been around almost continually since the late 1970s, there is a good chance that the car you want to purchase has a rebate program or will have one in the future. You can call around to different automobile dealers and ask what rebates exist, or check the car ads in the classified section of your local paper. Many ads will read something like, "Only $12,997, after $1,600 factory rebate." Watch for them. About 12 to 15 million new cars and trucks are sold in this country annually. You might as well get money back the next time you buy one!

How Much You Can Raise

This depends on which car you want and what rebate programs are in effect at the time you are ready to purchase. If none are in effect at the moment, it makes sense to wait until a rebate program comes along because the amounts you can receive are substantial. Rebates on smaller, less expensive cars usually start at $800 to $1,000. They can go as high as $4,000 to $5,000 on the more expensive automobiles (which cost $15,000 to $25,000).

How Fast

In some rebate programs, you get a company check the day you buy the car. In others, the dealer sends in the paperwork and you receive your money in four to eight weeks. You may also have to wait for a rebate program if none is in effect at the time you want to purchase your new car.

CREDIT NEEDED

The better your previous credit, the less money you will have to put down in order to get a car loan.

ADVANTAGES

Who wouldn't want to get money back after buying a new car? Automobile rebates are a simple, no-hassle way to make money. There is no borrowing involved, although your loan amount and your car payments would be lower if you had applied the rebate toward the down payment. A rebate may even allow you to buy a new car with no cash down payment whatsoever, allowing you to keep your money in savings to use for other purposes.

DISADVANTAGES

With rebates, timing is everything. Rebates come and go, increase and decrease, with amazing speed. Even dealers get confused sometimes because there are so many programs! Since a rebate program may not be in effect at the time when you choose to buy your new car, you may have to wait. Also, a little negotiation is required on your part in order to keep the rebate from becoming a dealer discount. *It is not!* Although dealers are sometimes required to participate in some small way with the factory, generally rebates don't cost dealers a penny.

#52. Money Back on Your Trade-In

Before reading this chapter, make sure you have read and understood number 51, entitled, "Keep The Rebate!" because the principles here are the same.

Probably about half of all people who buy new or used cars from car dealers have trade-ins. A trade-in simply means using your old car as a down payment on a new one. If you are using a trade-in, do you realize that you may be able to get cash back from the dealer? It takes a little negotiating, but it can be done. As a matter of fact, it is often done by astute buyers.

Here's what you do. Let's say that you are buying a new car for $10,000 plus the tax and license fees. The car you want to trade in is appraised by the dealer for $2,500. You can ask the dealer to give you a check back for $1,500 as a condition of the sale and apply only $1,000 to the down payment. As long as there is enough equity left over to satisfy the bank and allow the deal to fly, the dealer will go along with your request.

Often, buyers are unaware that they can get money back when they trade in a vehicle, and they end up making very large, unnecessary down payments (in the amount of their entire trade-in value)!

This is also a good way to reduce your outgo if you are trying to lower your bills a bit. Even if you are still paying for your present car, you may be able to trade it in for a less expensive car, using the equity in your present car to pay off the new car in full, thereby eliminating one of your monthly payments.

How Much You Can Raise

This depends on the appraised value of your car, and how little you can talk the dealer into using for the down payment. If your trade-in is worth $5,000 and the dealer will accept $1,500 as the down payment on the new car, you can receive $3,500 back.

How Fast

A dealer will probably not cut a check for you until the entire deal is approved by the bank. This may take as little as two days or as long as ten days.

Credit Needed

The better your credit, the smaller the down payment necessary to make a deal work.

Advantages

The major advantages are the same ones as those in number 51 regarding rebates. Another advantage is that you don't have the aggravation of selling your old car on your own before buying a new one, and you still get cash out of the transaction.

Disadvantages

Again, look at number 51 for the disadvantages. One other

disadvantage is that a dealer may offer you $1,000 or $2,000 less for your car than you might have been able to get by selling it privately. It may be more worthwhile to sell your present car first, then put down a small down payment on the new car and bank the difference.

#53. Take Your Vacation Pay

Most employers offer you a week or two of paid vacation after you have been employed for a couple of years. Many companies offer even more; some give four or five weeks of paid vacation per year after a certain number of years of employment. This is no secret, but you may not know that you can take your vacation money in cash rather than taking time off and getting paid.

Let's say that you earn $700 per week, and you have two weeks of paid vacation coming. You may be able to take the $1,400 in cash rather than taking the time off from your job. To find out if your employer will allow this, talk to your company controller, payroll clerk, or benefits manager.

While it's always fun to take time off, this could be a great way to raise some cash without having to borrow.

How Much You Can Raise

This depends on how much you earn and how many weeks of paid vacation you have coming. Check it out with your employer. You may have thousands of dollars available to you in this way.

How Fast

Obviously, you have to have worked somewhere for more than a year or two in order to be eligible for vacation pay. Also, your vacation pay may be available only on the anniversary of your hire date. Once that day has arrived, you should be able to get the money on the following payday.

Credit Needed

Your credit rating doesn't matter.

Advantages

The big advantage to taking your vacation pay rather than a vacation is that it is a great way to raise cash without borrowing. The money is available to you without any effort on your part. No extra overtime, no part-time job.

Disadvantages

There are three main problems with taking your vacation pay. First, your employer may not allow it. You may have to take the time off in order to receive your money—in which case, you're not getting any extra money, you're simply getting your regular pay while you're off work. Second, the money may not be available at the time when you need it. And third, it is good for you to take time off from your job. This is why your employer may want you to take time off instead of just taking the cash and remaining on the job. You can get pretty burned out if you never take time off to recharge your batteries. For this reason, I wouldn't use this method every year.

#54. Take Your Employee Buyout Incentive

As our economy slows down, more and more companies are downsizing by selling divisions and laying off workers. Many of these corporations, in effect, "bribe" employees to quit rather than laying them off or firing them. These incentives to quit can be quite substantial and may be well worth taking, even though you would have to change jobs.

Typically, these incentives include one week's salary for every year you have been with the company, along with all accrued vacation and other benefits in cash. Also, your company will allow you to cash in all your stock or other pension benefits immediately. There may be some other miscellaneous benefits offered by your company. Altogether, these payouts can be pretty lucrative.

In 1986, a friend of mine was offered this kind of program by AT&T, which had been broken up into several regional phone companies. After only six or seven years with the company, his payout came to over $8,000! He had planned to leave his job anyway and take one with AT&T's competitor, MCI. For him, and for thousands of others, these company termination incentives work out nicely. Many people even use the money to begin their own businesses!

How Much You Can Raise

That depends entirely on how long you have been with your company, what your salary level is, and how lucrative your companies' incentives are.

How Fast

If you decide to take advantage of it, you can receive your money in about a week or two.

Credit Needed

Your credit rating doesn't matter.

Advantages

No one likes to switch jobs, but if you were planning to quit, retire, or begin your own business anyway, taking your termination incentive may make a lot of financial sense. If you have been with a company for a long time, your payout may be $20,000 to $50,000! That's quite a nice little nest egg to sit on while you plan your future!

Disadvantages

The problem with taking an employee buyout incentive is that you may not want to quit, regardless of how much cash you could walk away with. Also, your company may not offer this kind of program, or may not offer it when you are prepared to take it. If you do take this type of payout, invest the money rather than spending it on a good time. After all, a portion of your payout may be part of your retirement benefits. Use it wisely!

#55. Factoring

If you own a business and a lot of your money is tied up in unpaid receivables, you may be able to raise cash through factoring. Factoring simply means selling off your cash receivables to a bank or investor at a discount or getting a loan from them, using the receivables themselves as collateral.

Let's say that your business has $25,000 in receivables due from your customers in the next sixty days, but you need the money now to pay off other bills. You can sell off your unpaid receivables for a discount of 5 to 8 percent. In other words, by factoring you could get $23,000 to $23,750 in cash, immediately, rather than waiting thirty to sixty days for the full amount. Or you could get a loan using your receivables as collateral. The interest rate on these loans is usually 2 to 4 percent per month.

You can find lenders who make this type of loan by looking in the Yellow Pages under "Factors," or under

"Loans" for banks offering receivable loans. You can also find factors in the "Business Loans" section of most metropolitan newspapers.

How Much You Can Raise

You can get a loan for the full amount of your receivables or sell them for immediate cash at a 5 to 8 percent discount (depending on the age and quality of your receivables).

How Fast

You can have the money in a couple of days.

Credit Needed

Factors are more concerned about your customers' ability to pay, since they are the ones who will actually be repaying the loan.

Advantages

Factors come in to play when you have exhausted some of the more conventional sources of funds. Factors will loan you money against your receivables, while most banks require hard assets as collateral. If your receivables are shaky, it may make sense to get 92 to 95 percent of their value now rather than take a chance of losing them completely later (if they can't or won't pay). If you plan to use factors to raise cash, you may be able to build in their discount up front, so you can actually let your customers pay the discount.

Disadvantages

The main disadvantage to using factors is the high rate they charge. You may not have enough profit to give up 5 to 8 percent to get the money now. Also, if you use factors for loans against your receivables, they may want additional collateral that you may not be able to provide.

#56. Buy, Fix Up, and Resell

This cash-raising idea takes a little time and money, but it has some excellent benefits. The basic plan is to buy something at a low price (such as a car, motorcycle, tractor, or small boat), repair it, clean it up, then resell it.

I know from my own experience in automobile sales that often you can buy a car cheap, spend some time detailing it, and make hundreds, sometimes thousands of dollars more when you sell it. Just by cleaning it up! The main thing most people look at when deciding to buy a car is its appearance. If a car looks good and runs reasonably well, it will sell. Most people equate the appearance of the car with its mechanical condition.

To begin, simply look for low-priced cars in the ads of your local papers, or look for cars that are parked with "For Sale" signs in their windows. Try to find one that is in good mechanical condition but looks in need of a good cleaning. Negotiate the lowest price possible with the owner. The less you pay now, the larger your profit will be later when you sell—and believe me, the guy who buys it from you will certainly dicker over the price. So don't you be afraid to!

Buy the car, wash it, clean the interior, steam clean the engine, and put Armor-all or some other sealant on the upholstery and tires. Sometimes a good detail makes a car look like new. Then put an ad in the paper at a higher price. When it sells, you recoup your original investment and make a nice profit. The amount of your profit depends on how much you paid initially and how much you can reasonably charge once the car is fixed up. That's why it makes sense to buy cars that are priced below market value. If you have mechanical skill, you could make even more money by buying cars that don't run, then repairing and selling them. This is more profitable, but it takes more time, labor, and investment. As a novice, it may be wise to stick with cars that just need to be cleaned up, not rebuilt.

I have talked mainly about cars, but you can use this plan on just about any type of vehicle—motorcycles, motor homes, trailers, boats, and the like. The same idea applies. Buy it, fix it up, then resell it at a higher price. Your profit is your "sweat equity."

HOW MUCH YOU CAN RAISE

Using this system, it's easy to make several hundred dollars. On more expensive cars (and as you gain more experience), you may be able to make over a thousand dollars on every car you recondition.

HOW FAST

Carrying out this idea takes one to four weeks or so from start to finish. You need to find the right cars, clean them up, then readvertise them for sale.

CREDIT NEEDED

Since you will generally be using your own funds, good credit is not a requirement.

ADVANTAGES

Anytime you can make extra money without borrowing, it's a good idea. You can use this plan anywhere in the country, at any time of year. There is no real space requirement—you could do your detailing in your garage, or in your driveway. If you are really good at this type of buying and reselling, you could turn it into a second job or even a career. In the automobile business, there are people called wholesalers who do nothing more than buy cars at one dealership, clean them up, then resell them at another dealer, and they make a few hundred dollars or more on each one. Cal Worthington, now a major Southern California car dealer, started out just this way about forty years ago.

DISADVANTAGES

You may not like working on and cleaning up cars and boats. Also, you need a small amount of cash to begin. (If you want to try this but don't have the money to begin, you could make a deal with the current owner of a car to clean up his car and sell it for him, and split the extra profit.) You may not be able to resell a car as quickly as you want to. That could tie up your funds for a while. There may be laws in your state regarding how many cars you can sell in one year. Selling more than a certain number may require some type of license. But if your buying and reselling really took off and became very profitable, it might be well worth it!

#57. Secured Credit Card

If you have had credit problems in the past, one way to reestablish your credit is to apply for a secured credit card (usually MasterCard or VISA). With a secured credit card, you keep a certain balance on account with a bank, and it gives you a card with that same credit limit. For example, you deposit $500 with the bank, and it gives you a VISA card with a $500 limit. The bank is protected because it has your money on account, and it charges you 21 percent interest on your credit balance. You come out ahead because you get a chance to reestablish your credit, and you usually earn interest on the money you keep on account at the bank.

This is not a way to raise extra cash per se, but if you have a poor credit record, any bank that will grant you credit is a godsend! And if you pay your balance on time, you start rebuilding a good payment record, which can lead to more credit in the future.

Listed below are four major banks that offer secured credit cards. I am not recommending any one of them specifically. (Your own local banks may offer the same program—check around.) Call or write each bank for its information packet. Pick the one that works best in your financial situation.

Bank of Hoven
c/o Service One
Credit Card Center
P.O. Box 9068
Van Nuys CA 91499-4009

First National Bank of Marin
946 Calle Amanecer, Suite M
P.O. Box 3696
San Clemente CA 92672-9815
(800-552-8985; in California call 714-492-2621)

Access Financial Services, Inc. (New Era Bank)
One Martin Avenue
Cherry Hill NJ 08002
(609-488-5252)

Key Federal Savings Bank
626 Revolution Street
Havre de Grace MD 21078
(301-939-0016)

How Much You Can Raise

Most banks require a minimum $250 deposit to receive a secured VISA or MasterCard, up to a high of about $2,500. Your credit limit is equal to the amount you keep on deposit at the bank.

How Fast

You can get your card usually within three or four weeks.

Credit Needed

Even if your credit is really awful, you can probably still get a secured credit card.

Advantages

If you have bad credit, this is one of the best ways to get reestablished. It forces you to keep a small amount of cash in the bank, which is good discipline for some people. You receive interest on your bank balance. Since the limits are generally low, it keeps you from going wild and getting in over your head again financially.

Disadvantages

First, you may not have extra money to keep in the bank. Second, the interest rate charged is the legal maximum (around 21 percent). Third, you have to pay an annual fee of $25 to $50 for the privilege of owning a secured card. While a small annual fee may not be unreasonable, a $50 fee on a $500 card is a bit steep.

#58. Cash from Your Customers

Every time you prepay a newspaper, magazine, or newsletter subscription, or pay for an item before delivery, you are in effect "loaning" money to that business. If you own or want to start your own business, you can use this same process to greatly increase your cash flow.

Having customers pay for an item before it is actually delivered is a way for businesses to increase their working capital with no interest costs whatsoever. Instead of trying to raise money for your business by using high-interest loans, you can use this means of getting your customers to give you the money interest-free. Your business will have full use of the funds, for any purpose, at no cost, until it actually delivers the product.

For example, if I pay $25 for a magazine subscription, the magazine has my money, and I have a promise from the publisher that it will deliver the next twelve issues of the magazine. In the meantime, it can use my money, and the money from perhaps millions of other subscribers, for any purposes it deems necessary, and those increased funds cost it nothing in interest.

Now, the magazine has to have a good enough track record for me to trust them to deliver the goods—the issues—to me as promised in exchange for my money up front. Also, it may have had to, in effect, "bribe" me to pay in full now for my monthly issues instead of just buying them at the newstand every month. The bribe could be a much reduced price (one-half the regular newstand price!) for paying in full now, or some other premium gift.

I have used a magazine as an example, but the "Cash from your Customers" idea could work in just about any business. There are hundreds of other examples: insurance, service contracts, most "service" type businesses, and so on.

In just about any business you want to get into, you may be able to have your customers prepay for your services, raising large amounts of cash with no borrowing whatsoever. The customer may not even have to pay in full for you to use this concept. Let's say you own an automotive repair shop. If a customer rolls in for a transmission job, you might be able to collect a $200 or $300 deposit to get the work started, the balance due when the customer picks up the car. His money, and the combined deposits from many others, could amount to a quite substantial sum, even before any of the work is completed. It could cover all your parts and labor costs, reducing the amount of cash you need from other sources.

How Much You Can Raise

Ideally, you could raise tens of thousands of dollars from your customers—possibly even enough to get your business going with no outside financial help.

How Fast

You can get this cash immediately—as soon as your first customer walks through the door.

Credit Needed

You don't need good credit to make this plan work—only a reputation for keeping your word and doing quality, on-time work.

Advantages

The advantages of this plan are obvious. Instead of groveling to your local banker for a loan for working capital, you simply have your customers provide the loan interest-free in the form or prepayments and deposits for goods and services ordered. Or you can use your customers' prepayments as a cash source to expand your business.

Disadvantages

Using customers' money before finishing a job is risky, because unforseen circumstances may keep you from completing the job. If you have already spent the money but cannot complete the work required, you may be in for a lawsuit. The idea is to use the money wisely. Use it only as you are completing the work. That way you are simply covering your own costs as they come due.

#59. Sell Your House

I have saved this method of raising cash for the end of the book because it is one of the most drastic. Most people don't regard their house as something to be sold in order to raise cash. Their house is like their wedding ring. They would almost rather starve than sell it.

Well, there come times when a house is more of a burden than a benefit. If you have lost your job, face a major illness, or are retiring and don't need such a large house anymore, your house can be turned into a giant cash source. As a matter of fact, most of the net worth of the average person in this country is tied up in his home. If you can cut out the emotional attachment, selling your home may be an excellent source of money.

If you are getting into financial difficulty, don't be afraid to sell your home and use the equity to pay off other debts. One of the reasons that there are so many foreclosures in the United States is that people tend to wait until the last minute to sell their home to raise money. After they have waited so long, there often isn't time to sell the home and go through the escrow period, so they end up losing the home *and* their equity in foreclosure.

If you are ready to retire, you may have built up hundreds of thousands of dollars in equity in your home. Your kids are gone, so you don't need such a large house. You can sell your large home, pay cash for a much smaller home or condo or mobile home, and put the rest of the money in the bank as a source of income for the future. The government actually encourages you to do this by giving you a one-time tax break on the capital gains on your home sale if you are fifty-five or older.

If you have lost your job or are facing a major illness or other emergency, sell your home and use the money as a cushion until you can get back on your feet again. It is much better to sell your home and receive the equity now than to wait and possibly lose your home to foreclosure if you get behind in your payments. If you can't make your payments, the lender will eventually foreclose. You will have to leave your home, and you will lose all the equity you had in it. It's always better to work out your plan of action when you are in control of the situation and are not desperate for cash. You can always buy another house and start all over again after the crisis is over.

Or maybe you're not facing retirement or unemployment, but you want to raise a large amount of cash to start a business. If you cannot raise the necessary funds in any other manner and if you are sure of the success of your business, sell the house and use the money for initial startup funds.

Selling your home may be a gut-wrenching experience, but in many cases it makes a lot of sense!

How Much You Can Raise

This depends on the equity you have built up in your home, but it could come to hundreds of thousands of dollars. You may want to try to sell your home yourself and save the 5 to 6 percent fee that most real estate salespeople charge. There are dozens of books at your local bookstore on how to sell your home yourself, how to get more money for it, and so on. It may be worthwhile to read up on the subject if you plan to sell your home to raise cash in the future.

How Fast

This process is not very fast. It may take one to six months to sell your home, and it may take another thirty to sixty days to close your escrow. Do yourself a favor—if you see that you are getting behind and may need to sell your home, don't wait. Get started immediately.

Credit Needed

Your credit rating doesn't matter.

Advantages

The main advantage to selling your home is the large amount of money that you may be able to raise. For most people, the majority of their wealth is tied up in their home equity. If you borrow against your home, you can usually get only up to 80 percent of the appraised value. By selling your home you get 100 percent of the value in cash (minus the sales commission and other closing costs). This 20 percent difference may equal $20,000 to $50,000! Don't be afraid to sell. In many cases, such as retirement, it may make good economic sense.

Disadvantages

It's hard for most people to even consider selling their home. We all tend to build up an emotional bond with our house. This explains why many people lose their home to foreclosure, when they could have sold it months earlier, before their late payments got them in trouble.

When you sell your home, you will have to pay taxes on the profit, unless you buy another home of greater value within two years. So you can decide within the twenty-four month period whether you want to buy another home. If you are in financial trouble, this two-year period may be all the time you need to get back on your feet and start over. You could sell your home, use the profits, then buy another home within twenty-four months, and no capital gains taxes would be due.

If you are fifty-five or older, you get a one-time tax exemption on your house profits up to $125,000. This makes it easier for older people to sell a large home and move into a smaller one. Talk to your tax preparer or accountant about the tax consequences, since they change from year to year.

The last drawback to selling your home is that since it is such a large source of cash, you don't want to squander it. Sell your home to raise cash only if it makes good financial sense.

#60. Always Have a Backup Plan!

No matter which plan you are using to raise money, always pick a backup or secondary source of funds in case your main plan doesn't work for some reason. There is nothing worse than waiting several weeks or even a couple of months for money to come, then have a problem at the last minute.

Choose your primary money-raising plan, then choose a second—even a third and fourth—source, in case the first one fails. Work on several plans at the same time. At worst, you've lost some extra time. At best, you may raise a lot more money that you needed. You don't have to experience that gut-wrenching feeling when Plan A fails. You've thought ahead and have Plans B, C, and D ready to go.

IN CLOSING . . .

Dear Reader,

If you liked this book (or even if you didn't) and have suggestions for improvement, I'd like to hear from you. If you know of other ways to raise cash fast that we haven't used, please send them in. If we use them in our next edition, we'll give you credit for the idea in the new book and a copy of the new book. Send all correspondence to:

Cris Molles
P.O. Box 1766
Lomita CA 90717